HLY HABITS

FROM THE

SACRED HEART

"If we want a strong Church, we need strong families devoted to the love of the Sacred Heart of Jesus, a devotion with roots that go back for centuries. This book offers concrete and practical ways of healing broken relationships within the family and experiencing not only the mercy of the Heart of Jesus but also the joys and delights of his Heart."

Bishop Earl K. Fernandes
Diocese of Columbus

"This book makes it clear that the Sacred Heart devotion is not some sentimental practice of piety from the good old days but is instead an important practice that can help families find hope in the midst of the struggles and challenges of today's world. In the Litany of the Sacred Heart, Jesus is invoked as the Abyss of All Virtues. Emily Jaminet takes several of those virtues and demonstrates through stories, reflection questions, and practical advice how they can help families and individuals find peace in the Heart of Jesus."

Fr. James Kubicki, SJ
Author of *A Heart on Fire*

"Even faithful families are a little dysfunctional these days. We all need the peace and direction that flow from Christ. With Emily Jaminet as our guide, we can recenter our hearts and our homes in the Heart of Jesus. Heartfelt testimonies, examples from saints and scripture, and her own experience will touch your heart!"

Fr. Joe Laramie, SJ
National director of the Pope's Worldwide Prayer Network

"A timeless treasure for Catholic married couples and families. Written from her own devotion and love of the Most Sacred Heart of Jesus, Emily Jaminet tenderly illuminates the virtues and graces available to marriages that welcome Jesus to reign in their hearts and homes."

Carrie Schuchts Daunt
Presenter and prayer minister
John Paul II Healing Center

TEN WAYS TO BUILD STRONGER,
MORE LOVING RELATIONSHIPS

HOLY
HABITS
FROM THE
SACRED
HEART

EMILY JAMINET

AVE MARIA PRESS AVE Notre Dame, Indiana

© 2023 by Emily Jaminet

All rights reserved. No part of this book may be used or reproduced in any manner whatsoever, except in the case of reprints in the context of reviews, without written permission from Ave Maria Press®, Inc., P.O. Box 428, Notre Dame, IN 46556, 1-800-282-1865.

Founded in 1865, Ave Maria Press is a ministry of the United States Province of Holy Cross.

www.avemariapress.com

Paperback: ISBN-13 978-1-64680-218-0

E-book: ISBN-13 978-1-64680-219-7

Cover image ©LeanneBowenFineArt, www.gettyimages.com.

Cover and text design by Katherine Robinson.

Printed and bound in the United States of America.

Library of Congress Cataloging-in-Publication Data is available.

CONTENTS

ACKNOWLEDGMENTS

I would like to thank Ave Maria Press for allowing me to publish another book with them. Thank you to the staff members and especially to my editor, Heidi Hess Saxton; she has become a Spiritual Sister in Christ and I am thankful for her encouragement to help this project come alive! Thank you to Karey Circosta, Heather Glenn, Kristen Hornyak Bonelli, Josh Noem, Stephanie Sibal, Niki Wilkes, Robert Harig, and the rest of the staff as well.

I would like to thank my immediate family including my siblings, in-laws, and extended family along with my nieces and nephews. A special thanks to my parents, who have taught me the value of hard work and working hard to share this devotion; my husband, who has shown me so much love over the years; and my children, who mean the world to me.

Special thanks to my Board of Directors, my volunteers, benefactors, ministry heads, and promoters of the Sacred Heart of Jesus, through the work I do serving as the Executive Director at www.welcomehisheart.com. I also want to thank Michele Faehnle, the Columbus Catholic Women's Conference, and the many individuals who shared their heartfelt testimony in this book. I love to share Christ's love with others. Special thanks to Fr. Jonathan Wilson (my older brother), Fr. Stash Dailey, and Fr. Joe Laramie, SJ; your priesthood inspires me to share this message with others. I cannot forget to thank my pastor Monsignor Moloney and Fr. Bill Ferguson and the entire St. Andrew staff and parish. I love my parish and children's school.

A special thanks to Bishop Earl K. Fernandes, Fr. Kubicki, Carrie Daunt, and those who have been willing to endorse this book. I appreciate your taking time to support my work. I want to thank St. Gabriel Radio, Relevant Radio, Spirit Catholic Radio, Mater Dei Radio, and the other stations that have hosted me on a regular basis to share about the Catholic faith.

I am grateful to those who have believed in me, supported me, and shared encouragement along the way! You have helped me to be a better person. Lastly, and most importantly, I thank Jesus, the Most Sacred Heart, and Mary, the Immaculate Heart of Mary.

A special thanks to the publishers whose works have been reproduced in this book as excerpts: *The Letters of St. Margaret Mary Alacoque: Apostle of the Sacred Heart* (1997 edition) and *Thoughts and Sayings of St. Margaret Mary for Every Day of the Year* (1988 edition) were both published by Tan Books in Rockford, Illinois. *Enthronement of the Sacred Heart* by Rev. Francis Larkin, SSCC, was published by the Daughters of St. Paul in 1978.

INTRODUCTION

Writing books is an amazing occasion to ponder the significant moments and influences in one's life. When I reflect on my own life, it is clear to me that nothing has been more influential to me than family—both the one I was born into and raised in, and the one I have created with my husband of twenty-four years.

For most of us, it is only natural to be influenced heavily by those with whom our daily existence is intimately entwined, and those with whom we share a bond of love. Ideally, these two groups overlap each other to a great degree, though tragically this is not always the case.

In any event, regardless of our experiences growing up, we can all find hope in something far deeper: whether or not we are aware of it, believe it, or claim it for ourselves, we are all born into a much larger family—the family of God. In this family, we are blessed with a benevolent Father whose love for us is infinite; the Blessed Mother, who reflects that love perfectly; and Christ, our brother, who offered his life on the Cross for us so that we might be happy for all eternity. Christians believe in a Triune God—the Father, the Son, and the Holy Spirit—and trust that, through baptism, we receive the Holy Spirit in our souls and are adopted into the family of God. Our inheritance is God's love.

One of the most amazing ways this love flows to us is through the Sacred Heart of Jesus. As we draw close to

Jesus's heart, which beats with infinite love for each of us, we are welcomed into the school of the Sacred Heart—a school of love where we learn the holy habits of virtue that enable us to let go of love counterfeits, such as the need to control and the tendency to love only with strings attached. In this school, we learn to welcome Jesus into the darkest corners of our lives so that, day by day, we build up a legacy of love within the family—the family into which we were born, the family within the walls of our own homes, and that larger family into which we were received through the Sacrament of Baptism, God's family.

THE SACRED HEART: OUR CORNERSTONE OF FAITH

I was born into a Christian family that extended for generations, each well aware of our inheritance as daughters and sons of God, each striving to pass that legacy on to their own children. Part of that legacy handed down to me through my family on my mother's side was a devotion to the Sacred Heart of Jesus. My mom described her earliest recollections of faith:

> Looking back, I can see that the Sacred Heart was the "cornerstone" of my family's faith devotion for both my parents and my grandparents and their families. Like the air they breathed, devotion to the Sacred Heart has filled our hearts and homes now for four generations. God kept his promises to our family through sickness, wars, sorrows, and joys. In life, they stood firm in their trust and faith, and in the end, they died confident that

Jesus was victorious, that they were dying in him and
his sacraments of love.

This devotion to the Sacred Heart wasn't a replacement for the fullness of the Catholic faith; rather, it bol-
stered that faith and provided a reinforcing framework
by which to practice it. Over the centuries, numerous
devotions to the Blessed Mother; the angels and saints; or
specific attributes of God the Father, his Son Jesus, or the
Holy Spirit have sprung up and have been practiced by the
faithful. Often, such devotions are introduced by a saint or
someone who has had a vision from God charging them
with spreading the particular message of the devotion to
address a pressing issue of the day. These devotions are
like signs along our journey, posted at particular points
in history to guide humanity toward its final destination.
Always, they point back to God and his greatness, typi-
cally to his great love for us, which is most often signified
by the heart of Christ.

Devotion to the Sacred Heart of Jesus is one of the
oldest devotions practiced in the Church and is considered by many to be "the" devotion because it centers on
the very heart of Jesus that beats out of love for us.

A Short History of the Sacred Heart Devotion

Jesus appeared to a French nun, St. Margaret Mary Alacoque, also known as the Great Apostle of the Sacred Heart
(1647–1690), in the 1670s. Drawing aside his garment,

he presented to her his flaming, thorn-encircled heart to reveal the great love he had for her and all of mankind and inviting all to make his heart their refuge and mediator between God and humanity.

While many have considered this to be the beginning of the Sacred Heart devotion, in his book *Love, Peace, and Joy: Devotion to the Sacred Heart of Jesus according to Saint Gertrude*, Servant of God André Prévot (1840–1913), a holy and well-known French priest and superior of the Congregation of the Priests of the Sacred Heart of Jesus, explained that the origins of this devotion can be traced back many centuries earlier. In the 1200s, St. Gertrude the Great shared an account of a vision she had of St. John the Apostle, who revealed that the devotion really began when St. John reclined his head on Christ's chest and heard the beatings of the Lord's heart at the Last Supper. In the vision, St. John told St. Gertrude, "My soul was penetrated with [the beatings'] sweetness even to the very center." He went on to share, "But to these latter times was reserved the grace of hearing the eloquent voice of the Heart of Jesus. At this voice the time-worn world will renew its youth, be roused from its lethargy, and again be inflamed with the warmth of Divine love."[1]

This powerful revelation by St. Gertrude is one small example of how many of the saints who embraced this devotion discovered a way to achieve holiness, through loving others as Christ loves us. These saints were willing to be vessels of love and allow Christ to lead them deeper into the abyss of love of mercy. The holy scripture comes alive when Jesus says in John 13:34, "I give you a new commandment: love one another." The love of Christ transformed past societies and can renew lives today. The devotion is truly our hope, for if we are willing to access the love of Christ, we can be Christ to others.

Let the Sacred Heart Renew Your Life!

When I look at the state of the world today and think about how the Sacred Heart has beat so continually for us over the centuries, I believe that Jesus more than ever wants us to come to him. He wants us—and our society— to rouse from our confused and distorted state and to allow our hearts to be renewed and restored with his love.

So often as I go about my ministry work, I hear numerous stories of pain and suffering, and I cannot help but ask, "Why should that time of renewal not be now?" The heart of Jesus needs to be rediscovered by our generation, honored in our lives and within our families, and shared with all of society. The love of Christ is not only for "serious Catholics"; it is the single most transformative force to change the world and set it ablaze with renewal and life.

Whatever your need, however much you and your family are suffering right now, the Sacred Heart beats for you. Jesus wants to come into your home and give you the healing and peace your family needs. A small step of faith—such as cultivating the holy habits we identify here—can help you begin to build up a legacy of love in your home.

As your faith continues to grow and you see God answer your prayers, perhaps you will decide to formally "enthrone" Jesus in your home; you can find more information about this in appendix 1 at the back of the book. For now, simply ask the Holy Spirit to show you where your home or your life needs to be renewed or restored. As he reveals these things to you, offer them to the Sacred Heart—just as so many of the people quoted in this book have done. Let their testimonies inspire you!

It is my hope that this book can be an instrument of renewal by helping you, through reflecting on the Sacred Heart of Jesus, to come to a greater awareness and appreciation of Christ's immense love for you. Each chapter includes teachings related to an aspect of the Sacred Heart, a testimony from someone impacted by practicing the devotion, a reflection on a related virtue, a section called Enter the School of the Sacred Heart that proposes ways to practice this virtue in your life so that it bears fruit and becomes a legacy for you to pass on to future generations, and reflection questions to help you allow the devotion to change your life. You could use this book as a personal devotional or read it with others in a faith-sharing group.

The Sacred Heart devotion is designed to give you not only supernatural hope but the graces you need to better love and serve God and others. Servant of God André Prévot wrote, "We are weak, but by the Heart of

Jesus we shall become strong; by the charity of the Heart of Jesus we shall, which is open, we shall find love, which is the source of all virtues."[2] May you experience that love through a deeper understanding of the Sacred Heart of Jesus.

1

RECEIVE THE KING: EXPERIENCE GOD'S LOVE WITH DOCILITY

Therefore, receive Jesus into your homes as a King, and a Friend. He is a King, as He Himself said with sublime majesty to the cowardly Pilate, and He desires that every family and every nation should recognize and proclaim His Kingship over human society. . . . He asks it of you as an act of reparation, and a consolation to His Heart. See Him stand at the doors of countless houses, rich and poor, crowned with thorns, His hair is wet with the dew of the night, begging and imploring to be admitted, asking for a shelter from the tempest that has broken out against Him in the world. . . . He is knocking with His wounded hand and saying to you: *I am Jesus, be not afraid, I am the King of Love, Open to Me!*

—Fr. Mateo Crawley-Boevey, SSCC[1]

WELCOME JESUS INTO YOUR HOME

Have you ever seen the famous William Holman Hunt painting *The Light of the World*, in which Jesus stands in front of a closed wooden door with no handle, knocking and waiting to be allowed entrance? The painting illustrates the scripture "Behold, I stand at the door and knock. If anyone hears my voice and opens the door, [then] I will enter his house and dine with him, and he with me" (Rv 3:20). This picture reminds me that I don't need to "straighten up" in order to welcome Jesus into my heart—or into my home. He wants to enter in to the messiness of our lives and assist us; he longs to be in the heart and home of every person, no matter their social status or place of origin.

What a blessing it is to know this! It is easy to practice our faith at church, but this faith of ours is not just a pious pretense, something we wear on Sundays and set aside as soon as we get home. No, we need his grace to live our faith in daily life and to change our habits. The Catholic faith transcends all cultures and social barriers and is meant to provide true meaning and purpose to all we do.

Before we can take the first step and welcome Jesus into our lives, opening the door of our hearts to him, we need to be able to identify his voice and build a relationship of trust and love. This ongoing relationship is essential to living out our Catholic faith, as without a personal relationship we miss out on the true meaning of our faith.

The Most Sacred Heart never enters by force; rather, with gentleness and kindness Jesus calls your name and invites you to the kingdom of love. Fr. Stash Dailey, cofounder and spiritual advisor of the Sacred Heart Enthronement Network, shares that "Jesus loves to rearrange the spiritual furniture of your home." He reminds us that Jesus often shifts our priorities and reveals what we need to know so that we do not stay in ruts and patterns that hold us back from experiencing the kingdom of God. Jesus doesn't want us to merely exist; he wants us to thrive, live an abundant life, and experience the kingdom of God here on earth. Here is my own story of transformation through the Sacred Heart.

Testimony from a Changed Heart

I can recall when the Lord gently touched my heart and invited me to experience his love in a new way through the Sacred Heart devotion. I was feeling burned out and overwhelmed by the demands of life. As a busy wife and mother of a large family, I knew I was running on empty and my love tank needed a supernatural source. I felt my limits and didn't know where to turn. I needed to find a true source of love that I could share first with my family, and then with others.

I am so grateful that, through this devotion, I experienced the kind of love that changed me from the inside out. I came to understand that before I could truly share love with other people (even my own family), I needed to experience this love myself! I can recall kneeling before my Sacred Heart image and saying, "Jesus, you can have my family, my future, and my life." Having said those words, I felt a total sense of freedom!

Over time, Jesus gently revealed to my heart the areas in which I needed to grow and change. After Jesus opened my eyes, I noticed that I was more open to the feedback of my family on areas in our life where we needed to improve. I started to let go and let God lead. After being instructed on how I was hurtful, I had to learn to say, "I am sorry"—not just with my words, but from my heart and with my actions. At first, it was hard for me to let go of my old ways, but my new way of living has brought fresh air to the home, and it even improved my marriage, as my husband was so grateful for my inner transformation. I notice that I smile more, laugh more, and don't take myself so seriously.

Jesus's love has no limits if we are willing to receive this tremendous gift and share it with others. I have seen what kind of impact it can have in healing hearts, cultivating a Christian home, and providing new purpose, direction, and meaning in life. I am thankful that Jesus's loving heart changed my heart.

LET THE LOVE OF JESUS RESTORE YOUR HEART

St. Margaret Mary wrote, "Love, glory and praise forever to the heart of our adorable Savior, which is all love, all loving, and all loveable, for all the good He will produce and work in souls by establishing the reign of His pure love in well-disposed hearts."[2] Would you like to experience the true and authentic love of Jesus Christ and allow him to heal and restore the dysfunction in your home? Jesus invites you to take St. Margaret Mary's words to heart so you can experience his true and authentic love. This adorable Savior is asking each of us to open our hearts to his truth so that we can experience his graces.

In John's gospel, Jesus said, "I give you a new commandment: love one another. As I have loved you, so you also should love one another" (Jn 13:34). He invites each of us to learn to have compassion and mercy first on ourselves and then on others, especially those who do not know better—those who have experienced love only from a place of dysfunction, who are merely giving what was given to them.

All too often, until we are open to Christ's love that flows from his Sacred Heart, our own dysfunctional ways hurt the very people we are attempting to love. Although our intentions might be good, our actions, words, and thoughts can easily wound those we care about the most. It is essential that we overcome our pride and see that the Lord wants to continue to form us and make our hearts like his. We must grow to be more sensitive to the matters that hurt God, to love others from a place of wanting what is best for them, to show compassion to others, and to be willing to forgive even when it is difficult.

Jesus wants to transform our hearts from stones to flesh! Listen to the words of the Lord from the prophet Ezekiel: "I will give you a new heart, and a new spirit I will put within you. I will remove the heart of stone from your flesh and give you a heart of flesh" (Ez 36:26). Through the Holy Spirit, a powerful transformation occurs; our heavy, burdened spirit is replaced with the new spirit of the Lord. Our cold and lifeless hearts, by the power of Christ, are set on fire with his love. Jesus is offering this transformation to each of us—a spiritual "heart transplant" to restore and renew our hearts. Why? So that we can be more like him and love the way he calls us to love.

Each of us struggles with matters of the heart. We have areas of our hearts that need a spiritual transformation. The transformation begins with admitting you have a heart of stone, or at least parts of it that are stony! When our hearts are "stone," we lack God's love and a sense of right and wrong, and we quickly justify our version of love, which can be misguided and confused.

Jesus desires to perform spiritual surgery in our hearts to repair the areas that are broken and wounded. These areas that are pain stricken need the love of Christ to pour out upon them so that healing can begin to take place. Jesus longs for us to allow him to touch our hearts so that we can begin to encounter true love. His love sets us free from our past and the lies that fill our minds and hearts, leading us away from God, who is love.

In a world that focuses on résumés and achievements, the Sacred Heart devotion can provide a spiritual transformation, for we are called to be open to the Lord and willing to live and share our love of Christ with others. St. Margaret Mary shared, "For Our Lord takes special pleasure in the efforts of the unimportant and humble of heart and abundantly blesses their work. . . . His grace works powerfully though gently and imperceptibly."[3]

Jesus wants to bless us and help us along this journey of spiritual growth in a gradual and gentle process of spiritual transformation. We must be ready to prepare a place for him in our hearts. Often the crosses and difficulties in our lives help gentle us and prepare us to remove the guards and shields we use as protection. But Jesus can't pour himself into our hearts if we are not willing to make room for him. Often, small steps can lead to significant and lasting long-term success if we make room for Christ. If we can make slow and steady progress in our spiritual growth or implement a holy habit, we will begin to see the impact it can have over time. For example, suppose you ditch a vice such as drunkenness, swearing, over eating, over spending, being rude and impatient with others, or even indulging in sinful media; it will make a world of difference in your life. The key to this life-changing transformation is that you allow Jesus to lead and help you cultivate new holy habits.

DOCILITY: A TRUTHFUL VIRTUE THAT FLOWS FROM THE HEART OF JESUS

Jesus is always inviting us to personal conversion and transformation to overcome sinfulness; we need to grow in the holy habit of docility—that is, "letting go and letting God"—as we grow in holiness. *Docility* is defined as "the willingness to be instructed or taught"; it is the opposite of stubbornness and inflexibility. As Catholic philosopher Dr. Donald DeMarco wrote, "The only thing the docile person wants to know is the truth. The roots of docility are in humility and self-knowledge, while its fruits are in realism and practicality."[4]

When we allow pride and stubbornness to blind us, it is easy to mislead ourselves and ignore the truth of which our hearts are convicting us. However, when we are docile, we can change and be instructed, allowing the Lord to touch our hearts, guiding us as our will seeks to conform to his, bending and swaying with the fresh breeze of the Holy Spirit. The Holy Spirit always invites us to be docile to the ways of the Lord. The more open we are to the Holy Spirit, the more he will work in us.

We can see firsthand how the Holy Family is the perfect example of holy, docile living. The Blessed Mother is a beautiful example of Christian virtue; she had supernatural faith, hope, and love that enabled her to trust in God's will even as her child was dying on the Cross. Mary was docile to the Lord: she was open to the instruction and teachings of Christ, and she surrendered to God's will to save his people through the death of his beloved Son. The Blessed Mother responded to the Annunciation with trust and even holy wonder as God invited her to be the Mother of God: "May it be done to me according to your word" (Lk 1:38). She was willing to allow the Lord to work not only in her life but through her in a way that created new life! Her "yes" has a name: Jesus.

That "yes," which affects all of us, is a beautiful example of how God respects our free will and of how our choice to serve freely and lovingly is the most excellent gift we give God. When the Blessed Mother agreed to be the Mother of God, she didn't get the road map to know what would happen; instead, she remained in a posture of docility, and in so doing showed us how to do the same.

Let us pray to Our Lady to lead us closer to Christ as we embark on this powerful journey toward being open to the Lord through his Most Sacred Heart. Jesus's heart formed under Mary's heart in her womb, and thus she is our greatest advocate in the kingdom.

Enter the School of the Sacred Heart: Open Your Heart to the Lord

In our technologically advanced society, we have instant access to so much useless and even harmful content. So many distractions make it easy to ignore and neglect our Catholic faith. And yet, as we enter the school of the Sacred Heart, we come to learn how to love God and others, which helps us to change our patterns of thinking, of learning, and of living.

The Most Sacred Heart invites us to experience his love, mercy, and compassion in a way that transforms our lives. The love that flows from the very heart of Jesus can heal any heart, any home, and even our world. This love is not a fleeting feeling but pours from the very heart of Jesus, and it has markers so distinct that once we experience it we will never be the same.

The gospels are full of ordinary men and women who met the Lord, encountered his love, and left with a great desire to follow him. Think of the Samaritan woman at the well who was converted through a single encounter with him (see John 4:4–42). Jesus spoke truth with love into her life, and with that, she left her water jar and ran back to tell everyone about the Messiah. It says in scripture, "Many of the Samaritans of that town began to believe in him because of the word of the woman" (Jn 4:39); this powerful exchange set into motion the conversion of many other hearts as well. Even though we never got her name, her story forever shows us how Jesus wants to set each of us free from sin, for no sinner is exempt from experiencing the love of God.

So how do we begin to take to heart the lessons from this school of the Sacred Heart? One way is to read through the twelve promises of the Sacred Heart, which Jesus gave to St. Margaret Mary (see appendix 2), and reflect on which of these promises moves your heart. If you would like to know more about these beautiful promises, be sure to pick up a copy of my book *Secrets of the Sacred Heart* (Ave Maria Press, 2020).

Jesus takes great pleasure in being loved and honored by his creatures. St. Margaret Mary observed, "He has strengthened me in the conviction that He takes great pleasure in being loved, known, and honored by His creatures. This pleasure is so great that, if I am not mistaken, He promised me that all those who are devoted and consecrated to Him will never be lost."[5] When we enter into the school of the Sacred Heart and seek to cultivate holy habits, we must first and foremost know that Jesus wants to pour his heavenly blessing upon us and build a true covenant out of love, not fear or intimidation—just like the relationship he built with his disciples and even with the woman at the well.

When we are willing to be open to the Lord and allow him to teach and instruct our hearts, we can set out on a new path. Let us take the first step today by pondering the virtue of docility—and asking the Lord to help us be more open to what he wants to teach us.

LET US PRAY: HOLY HEART OF JESUS PRAYER

As you pray this prayer, reflect on the state of your heart. Then ask the Lord to touch your heart as you prayerfully consider the reflection questions below.

O most holy Heart of Jesus, fountain of every blessing, I adore You, I love You, and with lively

sorrow for my sins, I offer You this poor heart of
mine. Make me humble, patient, pure, and wholly
obedient to Your will. Grant, good Jesus, that I
may live in You and for You. Protect me in the
midst of danger; comfort me in my afflictions.
Give me health of body, assistance in my temporal
needs, Your blessing on all that I do, and the grace
of a holy death. Amen.[6]

REFLECTION QUESTIONS

1. Reflect on the following scripture: "Behold, I stand
   at the door and knock. If anyone hears my voice and
   opens the door, [then] I will enter his house and dine
   with him, and he with me" (Rv 3:20). Is your heart
   open and ready to welcome Jesus?
2. How can you carve out more time, energy, and effort
   to cultivate a deeper faith life and be open to the Lord
   and his life-changing love?
3. In what area of your life can the virtue of docility lead
   you closer to Jesus?
4. How often does stubbornness and lack of docility lead
   you to hurt those closest to you? How is the Lord asking you to change?

2

WELCOME THE LIGHT: OVERCOME SHAME WITH FAITH IN GOD'S GRACE

[Jesus] intends to restore life to many by this means by withdrawing many from the road to perdition and destroying the empire of Satan in souls, in order to establish there the empire of His love.

—St. Margaret Mary[1]

ᴅɪᴛᴄʜ ᴀ ʟɪꜰᴇ ᴏꜰ ꜱɪɴ

When I was growing up, my mom explained to me, "If sin didn't look fun, no one would do it." Sin often has an entry point that draws us in with the seemingly innocuous invitation "Jump in, the water is fine!" All too often the temptation might seem harmless enough, just dipping our toes in to test the water. But once we jump in with two feet, the pain, suffering, and heartache that sin brings washes over us. This is the seduction of evil: when we deliberately sin and go against God's ways, our inner conscience is silenced and we can easily lose our way.

Even at this point, we are free to choose whether to turn back to God to wash and heal the wounds of sin, or to hide from him in shame. But it is a favorite trick of the evil one to tell us that what we have done is too much for God to forgive, keeping us bound up in the darkness of our guilt and shame.

Here is something you can know for sure: Jesus wants us to let go of the shame and blame we place on ourselves and to accept our human flaws and weaknesses. We all have them. We are all sinners. And yet when we humbly acknowledge our littleness, our sinfulness, the fact that we are helpless to save ourselves, something powerful begins to happen: as we begin to follow Jesus and allow him to work in our hearts, we discover that our lives have renewed meaning and purpose in his kingdom!

Jesus wants to welcome all of us into the family of God. He is always inviting us into a relationship. Jesus offers us a "new beginning," a way to rewrite our life stories. No sin is too great to hold us back from the love of God. Jesus is often addressed as the Divine Physician, for he can and will heal, especially our hearts. The Lord shows us through his active ministry work that he came to set people free of their afflictions and pain through encountering a relationship with him. We read in Luke 15:7, "I tell you, in just the same way there will be more joy in heaven over one sinner who repents than over ninety-nine righteous people who have no need of repentance."

It is up to us whether we respond and walk away from the sin that draws us in. But we can never give up sin on our own; we need Christ to help us overcome these behaviors that hurt our souls and inflict pain on others even while they bring us pleasure and power.

Through the ministry of the Church, Jesus offers us his graces, his love, and his peace so that we can unite our will with his will and thus grow in holiness. We cannot serve Christ without his help! The first steps are to be open to faith and to allow the Lord to pour his abundant graces into your life through the sacraments, especially through baptism, Confession, and the Eucharist. Yet often we are held back from growing spiritually by fears of what others might think of us. Here is one such story.

TESTIMONY FROM A DEVOTED HEART

I never wanted to look too religious. I just wanted to fit in, which was evident in the size of the images of the Sacred Heart and the Immaculate Heart of Mary that I chose to place in my house. They were tiny and represented my love for God. Looking back, I was still so worried about what people would say about me if I got "too religious" or appeared too devoted to my Catholic faith.

Yes, I desired the Lord to be in my life—and I also wanted to look and act in a certain way. I just hadn't figured out how to balance my work life, family life, and faith life in a way that worked on my terms. And yet I could sense a deepening of my faith, and several years after my reversion to the Catholic faith, I experienced a spiritual breakthrough: I decided to allow Jesus to be the King, Lord, Savior, and Friend of my heart and home. This was a significant milestone in my life! I still recall when I hired a handyperson to hang the images I now have in my house after I did the Enthronement of the Sacred Heart. The worker said, "In all my years of working, say some seven hundred homes, I have never been asked to hang images of the Sacred Heart of Jesus and the Immaculate Heart of Mary." He was from Africa and also was a believer who appreciated this extraordinary moment in my faith journey.

Now I can't imagine my life without the images of the Sacred Heart and the Immaculate Heart of Mary hanging in a prominent place in my house. And now I realize how short-sighted I had been at this time in my life, only wanting a "token image." I realize that faith isn't about compartmentalizing; instead, our faith illuminates our whole life. Without God, we are lost. Without our Catholic faith and the sacraments, we can easily drift from one thing to the next and miss out on true happiness.

—A Woman Whose Life Is Illuminated

ARE YOU EXPERIENCING "HEART BLOCKAGE"?

Jesus doesn't block his heart from us. He offers us his heart so that all of mankind can grasp and experience his love.

When he appeared to St. Margaret Mary, he revealed his heart in a way that not only drew this great saint in but also revealed his glory!

In the second apparition, in December 1673, St. Margaret Mary had this unforgettable encounter with the Most Sacred Heart of Jesus: "I saw this divine Heart as on a throne of flames, more brilliant than the sun and transparent as crystal. It had an adorable wound and was encircled with a crown of thorns, which signifies the pain our sins caused Him. It was surmounted by a cross which signified that, from the first moment of His Incarnation, that is, from the time this Sacred Heart was formed, the cross was planted in it."[2]

This tremendous testimony covers many important aspects of this life-changing devotion. First, imagine what it was like for St. Margaret Mary when Jesus showed her his heart in all its glory. We can only imagine the splendor of this moment for her, gazing at Christ's heart, the vessel that contains his awe-inspiring, immense love for all of humanity.

Second, as she saw the crown of thorns piercing his heart, she understood how much pain our sins cause him. Our sins hurt our Lord, especially if we do not seek his forgiveness. Our sins may produce temporary pleasure for us, but they can never bring us eternal happiness or true joy—and they often lead to pain and suffering as our selfishness and disordered desires damage others and our relationships. Only Jesus can bring us peace, love, and joy.

Unlike the "crash and burn" we experience from selfishness and disordered attachments, our desire for holiness leads us to lasting stability and authentic relationships.

Finally, as we contemplate the cross St. Margaret Mary saw planted and secured right in the middle of his Sacred Heart, we are reminded that Jesus died for our sins in order to set us free and open the gates of heaven. He came here to earth on a great mission: to bring as many of us as possible to heaven with him to live in his kingdom. Jesus wants to plant seeds of faith deep within us so that we can endure the most difficult moments and know that we are never alone.

This was Jesus's central message when he appeared in an apparition to St. Margaret Mary in June 1675: "Then discovering to me His Divine Heart, He said, 'Behold this Heart which has loved men so much, that It has spared nothing even to exhausting and consuming Itself in order to testify to them Its love; and in return I receive from the greater number nothing but ingratitude by reason of their irreverence and sacrileges, and by the coldness and contempt they show me in this Sacrament of Love."[3]

These two apparitions share the essence and importance of this transformational devotion to the Sacred Heart. Jesus is inviting us to discover his heart and to come to understand and comprehend how loved we are and how we can make up for the coldness and indifference of others. The purpose of this devotion is to cultivate a deep devotion to the heart of Jesus. Jesus is inviting us to not only experience his love but know that we each have a place in his heart.

Let Jesus Liberate You from Sin and Shame

The devil deeply resents it whenever another soul is released from the bondage of sin and loves to hold over our heads the sins of the past, attempting to deceive us into believing that we can never be free. While most of us regret our past sins and how we have hurt others, sometimes we listen to the lies of the enemy and allow shame to hold us back. True remorse motivates us to change, but holding on to shame prevents us from finding the freedom Christ died to give us. At welcomehisheart.com, we share that the Lord in his mercy and love seeks to liberate each of us from the chains that bind us in our day-to-day lives. Only the Lord can truly liberate us from whatever keeps us down in this life.

So when you are reminded of past sin, what will you do about it? Are you willing to bring your regret to God and tell him you are sorry? Are you ready to be set free from your sin through the Sacrament of Reconciliation? Are you ready to let go of sinful habits and seek to "sin no more," or will you let moments of regret and pain hold you back for the rest of your life? Jesus wants us to experience reconciliation, to break the bonds of sin and evil in our lives, but we must be willing to bring our sins into the light and allow Christ to strengthen us.

The Lord desires that we take a step forward in faith to move away from shame and sin and experience transformation through the love of Jesus and his Most Merciful Heart. St. Margaret Mary exhorted, "It seems to me that the great desire which our Lord has that His Sacred Heart be honored with a special devotion, is for the purpose of renewing in the *souls of men the effects of the Redemption.* He wishes to make this Sacred Heart, as it were, a second Mediator between God and men, whose sins have so multiplied *that it takes all His power* to obtain mercy and the graces of sanctification and salvation which He longs to impart to them abundantly."[4]

This idea of abandoning ourselves completely in his heart means that we are invited to let the Lord work and begin saying yes to God and his will rather than allowing our shame, sin, and fear to drive our life forward.

Faith: A Virtue That Flows from the Heart of Jesus and Sets the World on Fire

"If you want to win Him over so that He will take special care of you, abandon yourself completely to His adorable Heart. Put off all self-interest and work most earnestly and lovingly at the task He has given you to do, so that you may be able to say that His most holy will has been accomplished in everything in which He has made it known to you."[5] In this passage, St. Margaret Mary is describing in a nutshell the life of faith that is the great adventure God invites us to pursue. As we seek the Lord and learn to love him with all our hearts, minds, and souls, he grants us graces to strengthen us to follow him. Faith is not meant to be lived in a vacuum; it is expressed in how we live our lives. What we believe in our hearts influences what we read, what we watch, our attitudes, and even our lifestyles. Faith is not a spiritual "insurance policy" to cling to at the end of our lives. Rather, it is a lifelong journey lived out each day through our intentions and actions.

Once we have opened our hearts to Christ, sharing our faith with others—including our family—can be challenging. St. Catherine of Siena famously said, "Be who God meant you to be and you will set the world on fire." This fire is not a physical fire like a forest fire, but rather a fire of the love of God. We were created to love God, serve him, grow in our love for him, share his love with others so that they can experience the flames of love, and be grateful for all he has provided us. We are invited to stop offending our God and begin striving to grow in holiness.

As we persevere in living a life pleasing to the Lord, the seeds of faith planted in us at baptism and cultivated through the other sacraments will blossom in us. Yet we must nurture these seeds if we want them to bear fruit! I have found that when I put my total trust in God, he always exceeds my expectations and delivers the fruit of the kingdom in the form of inner peace and joy. I can't imagine a life without faith, as faith has become my total reference and anchor at life's most stressful moments.

Faith reminds us that we are never alone despite the trials and difficulties we are enduring.

ENTER THE SCHOOL OF THE SACRED HEART: TANGIBLE EXPRESSIONS OF FAITH

One important way to pass your faith on to those around you is through tangible expressions of devotion. One aspect of devotion to the Sacred Heart is placing an image of his Heart prominently in your home to be honored and to remind everyone in the home how his loving, merciful Heart wants to help us change—and even help us turn to him in difficult times.

Do you have any tangible expressions of faith in your home? Over the last fifty years, religious art and "holy reminders" have become scarce in many homes. At one time, every Catholic family would have a crucifix, rosaries, holy images and prayer cards, and beautiful artwork. These items are now hard to find; as one friend said, "I had just finished a huge remodel; where now would I place these religious items?" She wanted to have images that invited her to pray, but at the same time she "didn't want to look too Catholic," even in her own home. This tremendous inner struggle invites us to embrace our faith in a new way and trust in the Lord.

Living out our faith is not as simple as just believing and going to Mass on Sundays; our belief in Christ must penetrate our hearts and allow the Gospel to transform the way we live—including the space in which we live.

When we allow Jesus into our messy way of life, we can be set free from this world and love others as Christ has invited us to do.

"You are the light of the world," Jesus said. "A city set on a mountain cannot be hidden. Nor do they light a lamp and then put it under a bushel basket; it is set on a lampstand, giving light to all in the house. Just so, your light must shine before others, that they may see your good deeds and glorify your heavenly Father" (Mt 5:14–16).

We must let our light shine on others! Not only is our faith a gift to ourselves, but it is also a gift to strengthen others. Peter Kreeft wrote, "Faith is living and not dead only when it '"works through charity" (Rom 1:17; Gal 5:6)' (*CCC*, 1814)."[6] Surrounding ourselves with beautiful expressions of our faith, also known as sacramentals, as constant reminders of God's presence in our lives is an important way to live out our faith and trust in the ways of the Lord.

As Catholic parents, we also place sacred items in our homes to help instill faith in our children—not only to fulfill the promises we made at each of their baptisms, but to help them better understand their identity in Christ. Jesus wants them to be confident of their place in God's family, which they received at baptism. Each time we gather together to pray as a family or spend a few moments with Jesus on our own, these expressions of faith and charity help us to live out our faith and pass it on to others.

We are invited to fill the world with the light of Christ through our personal encounters with others. Our faith isn't meant to be something we hide; instead, we are invited to be transformed so that we are more like Christ—more loving, kind, and merciful. This is the secret to how to change the people with whom you live and work. Cultivating a more profound devotion to the Sacred Heart of Jesus allows our hearts to awaken so we can better love God and others.

LET US PRAY: PRAYER OF ST. BERNARDINE

My Jesus, You have loved us with all Your Heart, even unto death. You have unlocked Your Heart to us through Your open side. You invite us to enter into this unexplainable Love. Let us go then to Your Heart, this deep heart, this silent heart, this heart which forgets nothing, this heart which knows all, this heart which loves us and burns with Love. Let us enter, never more to leave. Amen.[7]

REFLECTION QUESTIONS

1. Pause and ask the Holy Spirit to bring to mind any unresolved sin in your life. Ask yourself: How have I dealt with past sins in my life—with regret or shame? Am I willing to let go of these past sins by bringing them to Jesus for healing?

2. When was the last time you went to the Sacrament of Reconciliation? If it has been a long time, or if you are conscious of serious sin, why not make plans to go as a family this week?

3. How are you a "light to the world"?

4. What tangible signs of faith do you see in your home? If you do not already have one, where could you create a family altar with an image of the Sacred Heart to help those in your home better experience the love of Christ?

3

MAKE YOURS
A HOUSE OF PRAYER:
BUILD FORTITUDE WITH JESUS

If I speak in human and angelic tongues but do not have love, I am a resounding gong or a clashing cymbal. . . . Love is patient, love is kind. It is not jealous, [love] is not pompous, it is not inflated, it is not rude, it does not seek its own interests, it is not quick-tempered, it does not brood over injury, it does not rejoice over wrongdoing but rejoices with the truth. It bears all things, believes all things, hopes all things, and endures all things. Love never fails.

—1 Corinthians 13:1, 4–8

Do You Love with "Strings"?

What kind of love do people experience in your home? Is your house full of disordered, selfish love counterfeits? Jesus's love is kind and gentle; he wins us through his loving ways. He wants to free us from dysfunctional love counterfeits, including those that we have slowly learned to accept or even justify from those we love. As we turn our lives over to him, the Lord begins to remove the distortions until, slowly, our hearts are transformed or retrained until at last they begin to resemble his pure and loving heart. Our relationships will thrive as our hearts become so inflamed with love that we become (in the words of St. Margaret Mary) "one with His Heart."[1]

As we take time out of our busy lives to reflect on the loving heart of Jesus, we become drawn into his heart and discover the great mystery of God's love. You see, the Sacred Heart contains the love of God the Father, the Son, and the Holy Spirit. His heart is where humanity and divinity come together and beat in unison. And when we enthrone the Sacred Heart in the center of the home, the beat of that loving Heart becomes a focal point of faith, strengthening us to endure life's difficult experiences: sicknesses, disappointments, estrangements, and conflicts can all be brought to the Lord for his healing touch. "But you, Lord, are enthroned forever; / your renown is for all generations" (Ps 102:13). If we are willing to give our hearts to Jesus, he can and will make all things new.

Here is one couple's experience with enthroning the Sacred Heart.

Testimony from Renewed Hearts

It took a long time for me ("Bob") to agree to the Enthronement of the Sacred Heart. My wife (let's call her "Ann") asked me a few times, and I would dismiss the idea each time. Although I was very involved in our Catholic faith, it just seemed like one more thing. However, looking back, I regret we didn't do it sooner—it represents a significant turning point in our lives. When we finally did the Enthronement of the Sacred Heart, we were amazed at what a huge blessing it was for our marriage and family.

We invited our older children, who are all out of the home, to be present so they could better understand our desire to welcome the Reign of Christ into our life publicly. Almost right away we noticed the difference it made in our lives; becoming more Christ-focused brought greater trust, intimacy, and sense of togetherness in our marriage. In addition, it greatly enhanced every aspect of our faith, giving it new meaning—from going to adoration and Mass, to saying our Rosary, to just sharing our faith with others in daily life. Since our Enthronement of the Sacred Heart, we have helped over a hundred other families go through the Enthronement process so they can also experience the many blessings from the Heart of Jesus.

—A Couple Blessed by the Sacred Heart

Four Steps to a Prayer-Centered Home

I can't speak enough about the importance of personal prayer life. Prayer is our daily source of strength; without prayer, we are unable to experience the graces and blessings the Lord wants to pour into our lives. Each time we open our hearts to the Lord and persevere in our prayer life, we will experience the riches God wants to bestow upon us. The prayer lives of the great saints, especially those devoted to the Sacred Heart, remind us of the harvest of great spiritual fruits for those who persevere.

Do you need a spiritual makeover? Here are four steps you can take to make your home a prayerful place where Jesus is at the center and the whole family is at peace.

1. *Display the Sacred Heart in your home.* The best, most powerful way to do this is by having an enthronement ceremony (see appendix 1 for more information on how to do this). This spiritual ceremony, when participants welcome the reign of God into their place of dwelling, is a powerful way to bring spiritual awakening to a family, a business, or a community. According to Fr. Francis Larkin, SSCC, "The Enthronement of the Sacred Heart in the home is a proven, effective way of creating the right atmosphere for prayer in the home, for actualizing the potential the family has for a stronger Christian family life; to bring the family closer to the Person of Christ in the Eucharist."[2]

We are invited to let the light of Christ into our lives through the enthronement and build a covenant of love. This act is not an empty gesture of piety and belief but a practical way to publicly acknowledge our love for Jesus, give our Lord permission to dwell with us, and welcome his kingdom of love. St. Margaret Mary once said, "He will shower them in abundance of graces every place where a picture of His divine Heart shall be set up and honored."[3]

When I was growing up, my parents welcomed Christ into our home through the Sacred Heart Enthronement, and the house was blessed by Fr. Losh, a family friend and priest. Our family's Enthronement of the Sacred Heart was a point of transition for our family as my parents came to appreciate that they needed to let go and let Christ be the actual head of our family. The enthronement was part of our family's "golden era of conversion" when my parents shed their worldly aspirations and focused on ways we could grow in our faith and as a family.

During the spiritual ceremony, Fr. Joe Losh opened the front door and said, "Satan, you are not welcome here; leave this house." Our jaws dropped at his declaration, yet we all noticed a difference after the ceremony. After that special house blessing and Enthronement of the Sacred Heart, our family home became more peaceful and Christ-centered.

2. *Be mindful of God's presence as you go about each day.* Looking back on my childhood experience, I can identify some extraordinary graces that were foundational for our family life. First, especially after our family enthroned Jesus in our home, I can recall an increased openness to faith experiences. Despite being "average teenagers," my siblings and I experienced a great deepening in our Catholic faith. Second, our home became more peaceful; family unity was a priority over just keeping

busy going from one activity to the next. St. Margaret Mary shared that "He is all-powerful to bring them peace, turning aside the just punishment our sins have drawn upon us and obtaining mercy for us."[4] The more we turned to Jesus in our day-to-day life, the more we experienced this peace.

3. *Look to the example of other, more mature believers who can help to guide you on your journey.* My parents turned their attention to the Sacred Heart devotion in no small part because of the example of my grandparents and relatives. They were incredible role models of Christian faith and devotion. My grandfather and grandmother were simple people who spent much of their time going to Mass and watching EWTN (Eternal Word Television Network), and my grandpa made his life a living workshop for Jesus. He converted his back basement room into a mini-factory for Jesus and Mary, where he would spend half of his day woodworking and creating plaques of the Sacred Heart and the Immaculate Heart for the Men of the Sacred Hearts located in Cincinnati, Ohio. This Church-approved fraternity of brotherhood sought to place Christ at the center of its members' lives and help spread the devotion to the Sacred Heart, including the Enthronement of the Sacred Heart. At one point there were local chapters across the nation. My grandfather assembled images, and they were shipped worldwide, including to Mother Teresa's Home for the Sick and the

Dying. Later my grandfather would make rosaries daily as he sat with my grandmother, who had Alzheimer's.

By his holy example, my grandfather taught us grand-children to be instruments for the Lord and to use our gifts and talents for Christ no matter how great or small they were, always with joy in our hearts and trust in Jesus. My grandfather's joy was contagious, and the love he had for his wife was extraordinary. I was blessed to have their example and that of other relatives, who all lived out the faith in a way that laid a robust foundation for our family to grasp what it means to be Catholic. Their joy and char-ity were infectious, yet at the time, I had no idea this was not everyone's experience concerning faith and family life.

4. *Commit to making sure prayer happens.* The more we make prayer a regular habit, the more we will expe-rience the fruits of cultivating a relationship with God. For example, I have noticed in my own life that when I rise before the rest of my house and set aside time to pray, I experience a more peaceful day and can "feel" the graces throughout my day and see the Lord in the small blessings. I have seen the spiritual benefits of giving Jesus my first cup of morning coffee. This quiet prayer takes place before my image of the Sacred Heart, and I think of it as a heart-to-heart with Jesus. During this time of prayer, I meditate on the day's holy scripture and share my prayer intentions with the Lord, including my fears, hopes, dreams, and those close to my heart, especially my family.

Over the years, I have noticed the value of praying many prayers of thanksgiving and praise, for his love is our greatest gift. Looking back, I see that my prayer journal is full of these prayers; I can see how the Lord has answered these petitions and the longings of my heart, drawing me into a deeper relationship of trust and friendship. After many years of this type of prayer, I feel empty if I don't spend this time with Jesus. The more I pray, the more I can detach from my will and desire to follow God's will.

FORTITUDE: A VIRTUE THAT FLOWS FROM THE HEART OF JESUS AND BUILDS A LEGACY OF LOVE

When we encounter a significant difficulty in our personal lives or struggle to dedicate some aspect of our lives to the Lord, the virtue of fortitude is what gives us courage to do what is right: "It enables one to endure difficulties and pain for the sake of what is good."[5] My mom often comments that even in life's most difficult moments, Christ was there. Our family was not exempt from suffering or heartache; but with Christ, "all things are possible" (Mt 19:26). When sorrow, sickness, and division hit our family, we followed in the footsteps of those who had gone before us and turned to prayer and the Sacred Heart devotion as a way to gain new strength.

My siblings and I were raised to experience Christ's love as an absolute priority, no matter how busy we were. We were taught to place Christ above sports, activities, our social life, and even friends. We went to Mass together as a family as much as possible, and every meal began with a prayer. If a family makes it their mission to share Christ's love with others, faith takes on a new dimension. Our family has struggled and still does, like all families. Still, the hope of Christ and the commitment to love like Christ has brought spiritual stability and hope, for no matter what situation we are navigating, Christ is always with us.

I also learned fortitude in my childhood because I was never allowed to quit a commitment just because life was hard. For example, I struggled to read and write as a young child, and this heavy cross later became a tremendous blessing as it built resilience in me and cultivated the holy habit of fortitude. I learned over the years to not give up and to encourage others to do the same as well.

How can you cultivate this courageous virtue of fortitude in your home? Fortitude is "the moral virtue that ensures firmness in difficulties and constancy in pursuing the good. It strengthens the resolve to resist temptations and overcome moral obstacles."[6] Fortitude enables us to conquer fear, even fear of death, and to face trials and persecutions in defense of a just cause. This virtue that flows from the heart of Christ strengthens us during times of great difficulty or uncertainty and helps us combat the daily fears and anxiety that can hold us back. Without fortitude, we can stand for nothing and will fall for everything. We will allow our emotions to dictate our actions and be easily dissuaded from doing the right (but hard or inconvenient) thing at work or at home.

We need fortitude to fight the tremendous spiritual battles we engage in daily, to face challenges at home or work without losing the strength of our convictions. We must pray for the fortitude to persevere, to withstand even great difficulties as did the great saints whose fortitude helped them stay faithful even unto death. For those who want lives centered with deep faith in God, the Sacred Heart devotion is a daily reminder of the Lord's desire to give us the strength we need each day to face what comes to us with fortitude and courage.

ENTER THE SCHOOL OF THE SACRED HEART: LIVE OUT YOUR FAITH WITH FORTITUDE

Families who enshrine the Sacred Heart image in their homes and commit themselves to the Sacred Heart devotion soon discover that this devotion offers a powerful way to live out the faith. If you have not already done so, I invite you to enthrone or renew your Enthronement of the Sacred Heart in your home in order to welcome the kingdom of God into where you reside and allow Jesus to pour new graces into your life.

As a devotion, the Sacred Heart is not a sacrament but a *sacramental*; it predisposes us to receive the graces God wants to give us through the sacraments. When we allow the Sacred Heart to enter into our messiness, even into our complicated problems, God can transform our hearts and home. The Lord doesn't want us to shut him out of our lives—not even the darkest and most embarrassing moments. Each time we come to him and tell him what is troubling us, he gives us strength to begin again.

Each generation has particular troubles and challenges; each faces circumstances that seem insurmountable or that threaten to crush us. Through the Sacred Heart, we are reminded to embrace the faith of our forefathers, the holy faith handed down from one generation to the next, and to begin again if we fall and stumble along the way. Whether our most significant trials occur within our own family or within the extended family, we are called to embrace fortitude in not only living out our faith but learning to share the love of Christ with others.

What obstacles are you facing that you need to overcome? Where are you being given opportunities to grow in holiness? How is Jesus calling you to lean on the Sacred Heart? Have courage to live out your faith in a new way and trust in the Lord.

LET US PRAY: PRAYER OF THANKSGIVING

Lord, you deserve all honor and praise, because your love is perfect and your Heart sublime.

My heart is filled to overflowing with gratitude for the many blessings and graces you have bestowed upon me and those whom I love.

Forever undeserving, may I always be attentive and never take for granted the gifts of mercy and love that flow so freely and generously from your Sacred Heart.

Heart of Jesus, I adore you.

Heart of Jesus, I praise you.

Heart of Jesus, I thank you.

Heart of Jesus, I love you forever and always. Amen.[7]

REFLECTION QUESTIONS

1. Where have you experienced love counterfeits that need to be purified with the love of Christ? How might the Sacred Heart Enthronement be a source of grace and healing?
2. Which of the four steps of the spiritual makeover do you need to focus on right now?
3. How can the virtue of fortitude help you grow closer to God?
4. How can you cultivate this courageous virtue in your home?

4

ESTABLISH CHRIST AS YOUR CENTER: FIND SPIRITUAL STABILITY THROUGH HOPE

Oh, how fortunate are those who can help with this work! They are thus drawing to themselves the friendship and eternal blessings of this lovable Heart.

—Jesus to St. Margaret Mary[1]

Rely on Jesus to Help You Do Good

One of the greatest fruits from this devotion is the spiritual stability the Sacred Heart brings to a soul. Jesus's most perfect heart can't deceive any soul; rather, he meets us where we are and leads us closer and closer to him.

Jesus invites us to develop a personal relationship with him and to experience his faithfulness. He is always faithful to us, even when we fail him out of weakness or ignorance. As the perfect teacher, he forgives us and continues to reveal himself to us so that we can grow in holiness.

To be devoted to the Sacred Heart is to live a life oriented toward goodness. St. Josemaría Escrivá wrote, "The task for a Christian is to drown evil in an abundance of good. It is not a question of negative campaigns or of being *anti* anything. On the contrary, we should live positively, full of optimism, with youthfulness, joy, and peace."[2]

This drowning out of evil begins with not allowing sin to be present in our lives. Where are the "windows" to evil open in your life? Does evil influence you through television shows you watch, your online activities, or the type of books you read? Does it sneak into your life through a selfish attitude or uncharitable thoughts? Evil is often disguised and begins in very subtle ways. But Jesus wants us to do good on behalf of the kingdom and to avoid evil and sin. These acts of goodness not only bear fruit for the kingdom of God but also provide us new purpose and meaning in how to spend our time and lead lives transformed by the Gospel.

Here is the story of someone whose devotion expanded beyond his own home even to the workplace. Are you in need of "spiritual stability" outside of the home? Let Jesus show you how to find it!

TESTIMONY FROM A TRANSFORMED HEART

The Sacred Heart Enthronement [see appendix 1] has been so helpful on a personal and professional level for me, my family, and my "work family." When we enthroned our home, praying together became a power-ful, transforming catalyst of change for our family prayer life. When we joined together nightly to pray the Rosary, it was so powerful.

Recently we just moved and renewed the Sacred Heart Enthronement in the new house. It was important to us to do something physical as a sign to our children that Jesus is the king of our home, and we wanted to make it very clear in the family that this kind of relation-ship with Christ is our common goal and at the center of all that we are and all that we do. When we enthroned the Sacred Heart in our business, we had such a shift in the core of our business. My business plan shifted, and the spa's focus became centered on Christ. Our core values and principles became centered on living out the will of God; it is such a shift. It made it more solid with the staff; everything I do is for God's glory.

Moving forward has been so fruitful. As a result of this decision, there was a complete shift in the culture of the spa we owned and ran. It forced some to leave our business who didn't want to live in the light and go along with the changes we made, including the type of music we played during the day. We didn't realize how much influence that darkness had on all of us until we were set free from it. Now everyone who comes here knows this is a Christ-centered business. This is who we are and what we do. This was life altering and made everything come to life; since then, everything has been focused on Jesus.

I am slowly learning to offer my crosses to the Lord when things don't go my way, such as when I have had some recent health issues and needed multiple surgeries. I see this as an opportunity to trust in the Lord, as his kingdom is welcome in my personal and professional life.

—A Business Owner Who Trusts in the Sacred Heart

Are You Experiencing Shake-ups?

Spiritual shake-ups occur when life heads in an unexpected direction, causing us to depend even more on the Lord; as the road splits, Jesus invites us to go through the narrow gate with him (see Matthew 7:13–14). By peppering our lives with prayer and devoting ourselves to the Sacred Heart, we can experience spiritual stability. When we forget to ground our lives in Christ in this way, we quickly give in to temptations and head down paths that lead us to lose hope.

Spiritual shake-ups can be like pop-up summer storms that we cannot ignore; these are the moments when we turn to Christ, repent, and choose to love and trust in his ways. These sudden showers can provide us with a fast track to change. For example, when a family member becomes sick or estranged, this spiritual shake-up reminds us that we want a Christ-centered family and drives us to our knees as we pray to the Lord out of our need.

What brings you and your family to pray? Is it a loved one who is sick or has been injured? Are you or a family member on the verge of a divorce? Has someone turned away from God or made life choices contrary to the faith? For many of us, our prayers out of need are opportunities to awaken us to the power of prayer. Hopefully, we make small steps during these difficult times to deepen our prayer life and depend more powerfully on the Lord. The shift begins with us turning to God and placing the troublesome issue in his hands instead of attempting to handle it ourselves.

When we pause and invite Jesus to reign in our lives this way, it is an opportunity for spiritual growth and transformation. In these moments, we give him complete authority to act according to his will. Despite our difficulties and weakness, the more we depend on the Lord, the more he can work through us. If we have troubled hearts and are experiencing difficulties, prayer can change our entire outlook. It provides us with supernatural hope, inner peace, encouragement, strength, and divine friendship and companionship.

This transformation process isn't always easy! Living the faith in a more intentional way can be challenging— just ask anyone trying to break a bad habit or take up a healthy new one. When we say yes to Christ, we need to be purged of the habits and ways that lead us farther away from him.

When we grow too comfortable, we can quickly lose our focus on the goals we set for ourselves, whether those goals are physical (like eating "clean") or spiritual (spending all of eternity with God the Father in heaven). And yet responding to the loving heart of Jesus must have a much greater priority than getting fit or losing weight!

As we seek to better live out our Catholic faith through responding to the loving heart of Jesus, we will be better able to love the people around us out of love for God. How we love leaves a lasting impression on others. Just think, we can know all the tenets of the faith, but without the warmth of love, our impression and impact is lacking.

The Lord is inviting us to make room in our hearts, homes, businesses, schools, and parishes for him. We read in Romans 8:28, "We know that all things work for good for those who love God, who are called according to his purpose." This process might include a spiritual awakening or even a shake-up, but our love for God is the critical ingredient for him to bring out good in all matters in our lives. So we don't need to fear that we are not good enough or that our past mistakes are preventing us from having a significant impact.

HOPE: THE VIRTUE OF SECURITY IN JESUS THAT FLOWS FROM HIS HEART

I have found that when I open my heart to the virtue of hope, I can better trust in the Lord and his ways. Jeremiah 29:11 was the first scripture passage I memorized, so that I would always recall that God is offering me a hopeful future: "For I know well the plans I have in mind for you—oracle of the LORD—plans for your welfare and not for woe, so as to give you a future of hope" (Jer 29:11). Hope is what should carry us in our dark moments; we know that God's "got this," no matter how severe or heavy the issue might seem at the time, for we are placing our trust in him.

A favorite T-shirt that I love to wear reads "Pray, Hope, and Don't Worry," a famous quote from St. Pio of Pietrelcina (Padre Pio). This shirt is a constant reminder for me that if I pray, I am filled with hope, so I don't need to worry about what is going wrong but rather can focus on cultivating a life of prayer.

According to the *Catechism of the Catholic Church*, "Hope is the theological virtue by which we desire the kingdom of heaven and eternal life as our happiness, placing our trust in Christ's promises and relying not on our strength but on the help of the grace of the Holy Spirit. 'Let us hold fast the confession of our hope without wavering, for he who promised is faithful' (Heb 10:23). 'The Holy Spirit . . . he poured out upon us richly through Jesus Christ our Savior, so that we might be justified by his grace and become heirs in the hope of eternal life' (Ti 3:6–7)" (*CCC*, 1817).

Jesus is offering us each a future of hope, especially when we make the Sacred Heart of Jesus our personal refuge. We trust him and believe that no matter what happens here on earth, our hope is always in Jesus Christ. He is our foundation and reference point, for Jesus leads us to his kingdom, a kingdom of love and peace.

A great example of how the Lord is always working and revealing himself is that the Supreme Court overturned *Roe v. Wade* on the Solemnity of the Most Sacred Heart of Jesus in 2022. This day took on meaning not just because it was the great Feast of the Sacred Heart, which is a "movable feast" on the liturgical calendar, but because in this particular year the Solemnity of the Nativity of St. John the Baptist overlapped the Feast of the Sacred Heart. St. John the Baptist is considered a forerunner of the Lord, as he proclaimed the divinity of Christ from the womb of his mother, St. Elizabeth (see Luke 1:41–42).

Now, some might see this overlapping of feasts to be some kind of "coincidence." But to this believer who has been praying, fasting, and placing her trust in the Lord for this intention, it was a divine sign. The last time these two feast days overlapped was in 1960—thirteen years before *Roe v. Wade* was even passed! When we are people of hope, we do not believe God has abandoned us or doesn't hear our prayers. This Supreme Court decision is a small example of how God continues to speak to our hearts during the times in which we live.

Jesus reassures us, "I came so that they might have life and have it more abundantly" (Jn 10:10). Without Jesus's graces, we are left to our own devices; no matter how we try, our love is lacking and self-seeking. If they lack hope, even Christians can quickly become pessimistic and believe that the best times to live were years ago.

But when we choose to live in the present moment and place our trust in Christ, he can redeem all things. God created us for this time, and we are invited to embrace the moment, not wish it away. If you allow the love of Christ to enter your heart and home, it will have a generational impact. As people of faith, optimism, and virtue, we see (and teach our children to see) the world through a lens of hope, with our eyes on our end goal, heaven.

This transformation comes out in how we speak of Christ to others. As we continually draw strength from God, we gain a new sense of confidence that we are not alone. This foundation creates security in our spiritual life and allows us to pass on this truth and hope to our children and grandchildren.

As people of hope, we are well aware of life's difficulties, but we place our attention upon the Lord and allow him to use us in our weakness. Our hope will enable us to "see that the difficulties of this life have a deeper meaning, they do not happen by chance, or by blind destiny, but because God wills them or at least permits them, to bring forth greater good from those situations."[3]

St. Paul tells us, "We know that all things work for good for those who love God, who are called according to his purpose" (Rom 8:28). These inspired words can ground us when life is hard and we are feeling lost. If we desire to foster the holy habit of hope, we must be willing to trust in God and know that the abundant life is a life full of faith, no matter what trial we are called to endure.

Enter the School of the Sacred Heart: Ditch Complaining, Embrace Prayer and Hope!

When life gets challenging, which it will at times, it is so easy and tempting to turn to complaining, which provides no spiritual fruit or benefit. Instead, it often leads to more anxiety and despair. It leaves us pessimistic and can actually harm our health.

Complaining might get the matter off our minds, but complaining isn't petitioning God. During prayer or seeking counsel from others, we are actively problem-solving. Complaining is one-sided, only looking at the matter through a human lens and ranting about our short-term view of the matter. Much of social media is now a platform to complain about everything from parenting to politics. Yet when we bellyache and moan, it doesn't bear fruit; instead, it leaves us worse off!

The Lord desires to work wonders and miracles in our lives and not leave us abandoned. When we encounter difficulties in life, they can become opportunities for us to grow closer to God and even to experience new meaning and purpose in all we do.

Let us go before the Blessed Sacrament and spend time in prayer, asking the Lord for the grace to be transformed by his eternal love. By his love, our hearts are set on fire, and we can gain the strength we need to allow holy change to happen by becoming people of profound hope.

LET US PRAY: PRAYER IN ANY NEED

Sacred Heart of Jesus, You have so often presented Your Heart as a sign of constant love between us. With utmost confidence, I point to Your Heart, which You took for love of men in the Incarnation, and know that You will grant me this grace which I ask of You. Amen.[4]

REFLECTION QUESTIONS

1. What behaviors, habits, and thought processes are holding you back from loving Christ and responding to his call to follow him?
2. Have you experienced a spiritual shake-up that has brought you or others back to the faith?
3. How can the virtue of hope change your outlook on life?
4. When you think of hope, who comes to mind and why? Who has taught you the value of clinging to this virtue?

5

CULTIVATE COMPASSION: AWAKEN CHARITY IN YOUR HEART

As for you entering into His Sacred Heart: enter in! What should you fear, since He invites you to come in and rest there? Is it not the throne of mercy, where the most miserable are the most graciously received provided love presents them in the abyss of their misery?

—St. Margaret Mary[1]

Just Come on In!

What prevents us from entering into the heart of Jesus? Just come on in! This saying reminds me of a young child trying to convince an adult to get in the chilly water to go for a swim. They just want that older person to "jump in, get in, please, just get in" as if they don't even notice the chilliness of the water. The adult might refuse to get in because of the water's temperature, which the young child almost doesn't even notice as their little chin chatters and their lips turn blue.

Is there something like that chilly water that is holding you back from truly embracing the Sacred Heart? As I once heard my friend Fr. Stash Dailey advise 1,700 men at the Columbus Catholic Men's Conference: "Get over yourself!" We need to take the focus off us and put it back on God. When we place the focus on ourselves and not God, it makes it more challenging to respond to Jesus's call to grow closer to him. But when we turn the control over to Jesus and let him reign on the throne of our lives, we discover great blessings. We will still encounter challenges and hardships—but these things, entrusted to God, will soften our hearts and give us great compassion for the struggles and sufferings of others. As St. Margaret Mary once said, "Provided He is pleased we ought to be satisfied, and ought not to be troubled about our feelings of dissatisfaction or annoyance; these arise within us only because we are not sufficiently mortified and simple-hearted to cut off the windings and reflections of self-love."[2]

When we place ourselves in the center of our lives, we are unable to love God or other people the way we were created to love. In the words of Fr. Mateo, "They seek peace, yet what peace can they have who do not adore, do not hope, do not love Me, I who am life? See with that indifference they treat Me, how they hold me aloof in all their life events! There are many homes where I have no part in the mother's tenderness, the father's care, or the children's affection."[3] Even today, homes lack peace, hope, and the love that invites us to be tender, kind, and considerate.

Jesus wants us to hand our hearts to him just as they are. Doing so allows us to take a full assessment of where we are, looking at our patterns of relating with others, and helps us grow. In the Holy Mass, we say, "We lift [our hearts] up to the Lord." That is precisely what Jesus desires, that we lift them to him and allow him to touch and change them. Listen to these words he speaks to each of us: "I am the resurrection and the life; whoever believes in me, even if he dies, will live, and everyone who lives and believes in me will never die. Do you believe this?" (Jn 11:25–26).

Here is the story of someone who discovered in the Sacred Heart a way to cultivate compassion for his own family.

TESTIMONY FROM A SOFTENED HEART

I didn't know I was challenging to live with, and I assumed I was showing lots of "tough love." This tough love involved lots of nagging and "inspiring" my spouse and children to do better. Looking back, I was hard on them, but I felt like it was for their good. I did my best to build healthy bonds of love between my children. Still, I was so easily triggered by their shortcomings that I lacked genuine compassion, preventing me from loving them unconditionally. This lack of empathy made me impatient and easily embarrassed by their behavior or appearances. Over time, I felt resentful for how my life was unfolding. I found it hard to trust in God's plan.

When Sunday morning rolled around, I was always full of negative comments. I never liked what my children wore to Mass, complained about being late, or found at least a few things to criticize. I thought the Mass was either said too fast or too slow, or I would recap the homily and judge the priest based on how he delivered it and what he said. Often I would rewrite his words in my head as if I could do better. I noticed everything and believed my way was the best way to live. When you are so full of yourself, it is hard to see at the time the impact it is having on others. I didn't think I had problems with others; I lacked perspective on "me" and the effect I had on others. I thought I was always helping others with my criticisms, but what I was doing was alienating myself from God and others. My lens for life lacked one thing—a heart like Christ's.

Looking back, I see the damage I caused in my relationships with people through criticism and negative statements. Now I focus on growing in virtue and being more like Christ. I am working on cultivating a deeper relationship with the Sacred Heart, so my heart is like his heart, and I realize that my opinions are just fleeting thoughts that often need to be reined in before they hurt others. I now desire to do the will of God and grow closer to Jesus through his loving, Sacred Heart.

—A Catholic Growing in Virtue

The Gentle Heart of Christ Can Soothe Critical Tendencies

St. Margaret Mary wrote, "But I am convinced that He wants to establish His reign through the gentleness and sweetness of His love rather than by the rigor of his justice. ... We must love Him with all our might and strength, no matter what the cost."[4] A critical spirit does great damage to souls; it tears down those around us and robs us of our own ability to enjoy life and live abundantly. However, the closer we grow to the heart of Jesus, the more our critical tendencies are rooted out as we are transformed in charity. We realize that we do not know the thoughts and intentions of other people, and that our harsh judgments are hurtful and un-Christlike. This realization is the first step to healing.

As we surrender ourselves to the Sacred Heart, Jesus's love first burns off much hurt, pain, and sorrow as we die to ourselves; then his love flows like a fresh spring of water, renewing and restoring us. With just one "splash" of the love of God, the Lord can begin to work within our hearts to heal us and show us how to use our gifts and talents for the kingdom.

If we focus on our own growth, we are less likely to be distracted by the faults of others. When we are critical of others, we miss out on the joy and freedom that the Gospel offers us. We are invited to embrace the virtue of charity and seek new graces so that the Lord can transform our hearts and develop in us a new way of looking at the world.

This transformation cannot help but impact our family. When we become open to our souls being watered by new graces, we become new creations in Christ, and even those closest to us may notice the change: how we speak, what we focus our time and energy on, and if we are bearing fruit in our day-to-day life. Have your children ever noticed a goal you worked on, such as growing in virtue, praying more, or trusting the Lord? These moments are awe-inspiring, for it means that progress is being made.

Charity: A Virtue That Flows from the Compassionate Heart of Jesus

Compassion is a spiritual muscle I have been actively building up in my life lately. As the mother of a large family, I can quickly become insensitive to the minor scrapes and bumps that my children experience or the pains they experience in their hearts growing up. I get in a rush, and in my eagerness to move on to the next thing, I forget to listen with the ears of the heart.

Showing compassion, especially to my family, requires me to slow down, enter into the situation, and practice "active empathy." My husband has reminded me over the years that "a hug would heal more than a lecture." When we show compassion and charity for and to others, we express a holy habit that will strengthen our relationships and allow us to be more like Christ.

When we lack compassion and are indifferent or apathetic to others, it is a sign that we have not allowed our hearts to be made soft through God's love. The Sacred Heart can awaken our hearts and help us to see our apathy and coldheartedness. Just think of how many relationships have been lost over apathy and indifference!

Before we can be compassionate with others or even with ourselves, we must first come to appreciate the love of Jesus's compassionate heart. The *Catechism* reminds us, "Charity is the theological virtue by which we love God above all things for his own sake, and our neighbor as ourselves for the love of God" (*CCC*, 1822). In scripture we read: "Though the mountains fall away / and the hills be shaken, / My love shall never fall away from / nor my covenant of peace be shaken, / says the LORD, who has mercy on you" (Is 54:10). Our God is a God of love and compassion, a God who desires not only to restore us individually to friendship with him but to restore relationships that have been damaged by our own uncharitable behavior toward others. We must ask him for the courage to forgive and be forgiven, so that our relationships might reflect the love of Christ to those who most need to experience it. St. Margaret Mary wrote, "I pray the divine Spirit of love to fill your dear soul with His most precious graces, and our hearts with the most ardent flames of His love, so that we may act only according to His inspirations."[5]

In Jesus, we have a God who has experienced first-hand what it means to be ridiculed and mistreated; he understands what it feels like to have a heart physically and spiritually wounded by others. And yet he has unfailing compassion even for those who inflict this kind of pain on others.

As our hearts are transformed by the compassionate Christ, we start to "see" with our souls as part of the spiritual growth process. We notice things we might have missed in the past, such as the homeless woman's eyes that seem heavy and tired, the cries of a child who wants to be consoled by their parent at the grocery store, or the older adult who is leaning heavily on her cane as she waits in a long line to check out. And when we let our hearts grow in compassion for others, we can better share this compassion with others. Just because we see suffering doesn't mean we are called to act at all times, but we can prayerfully discern what the Lord is calling us to do.

St. Margaret Mary shared, "He wishes to save many souls from eternal damnation, for their divine Heart is a fortress and a sure refuge for those fleeing from divine justice."[6] Jesus wants us to flee to his heart, a mighty fortress of love, so that he can save souls from damnation. Just think, Jesus is offering us his heart not just as a place where we receive graces and his love but also as a mighty, safe refuge where we go for security and serenity—even when we face "divine justice."

Why flee from divine justice? God is perfect; we are not. He will judge us accordingly, and our sins will be so evident and painful that we need Jesus to be our loving mediator between us and God the Father. We want to be part of his divine kingdom, where he is not only our king but our friend. Imagine being friends with the king, the Lord of the Eternal City and the Son of God. He wants us to run to his heart and come to know the love of our Savior. He wants us to grow in holiness and to become more like him.

We read in Matthew 5:48, "So be perfect, just as your heavenly Father is perfect." Jesus wants us to be perfect, not on the outside, as what we think an ideal family would look and act like; rather, this is about obtaining a perfect heart, a heart like God the Father's, full of love.

We can't fake this type of "perfect" the way we stage perfection on social media, but we can receive this perfection from God by being open to his sanctifying grace. Amazing, sanctifying grace is how we are transformed from the inside out. We don't just "fake it until we make it"; we admit that we need Jesus and that only through him can we be made holy and new. In the *Catechism*, we read that "the grace of Christ is the gratuitous gift that God makes to us of his own life, infused by the Holy Spirit into our soul to heal it of sin and to sanctify it. It is *the sanctifying* or *deifying grace* received in Baptism. It is in us the source of the work of sanctification" (*CCC*, 1999).

This free and wondrous gift of sanctifying grace, which each of us receives at baptism, has eternal consequences—and these graces continue to flourish and grow in us as we cooperate with them throughout our lives, asking the Lord to help us grow together in faith, hope, and charity.

ENTER THE SCHOOL OF THE SACRED HEART: LITTLE VISITS OF PRAYER

A great way to grow closer to Jesus is to visit your image of the Sacred Heart daily and connect with him through offering up small acts of prayer. I love to start my day with a hot cup of coffee before my family wakes up and pray to Jesus before my image of his Sacred Heart. I find that this time of peace and quiet is my favorite time of the day. I also try to recall our Lord and pause throughout the day to say small prayers like

- "I love you, Jesus"; or
- "I trust in you, Jesus"; or even
- "Jesus, meek and humble of heart, make my heart like unto thine."

When we pause and pray, we are able to refocus our thoughts back on the Lord. After we connect with prayer, we are called to serve and love others as we are serving and loving Jesus. We can do this by performing little acts of kindness throughout our day.

LET US PRAY: PRAYER FOR COMPASSION

Love of the Heart of Jesus, inflame my heart.

Charity of the Heart of Jesus, diffuse Yourself in my heart.

Fortitude of the Heart of Jesus, sustain my heart.

Mercy of the Heart of Jesus, pardon my heart.

Wisdom of the Heart of Jesus, teach my heart.

Patience of the Heart of Jesus, weary not of my heart.

Reign in my Heart, Jesus. Establish Yourself in my heart.

Let zeal for the Heart of Jesus consume my heart. Immaculate Virgin, pray to the Heart of Jesus for me. Amen. [7]

REFLECTION QUESTIONS

1. Which quote by St. Margaret Mary in this chapter inspired you to grow closer to Jesus?
2. In what area of your life do you most need to grow in the virtue of charity? What actions can you perform out of love to help you grow in this holy habit?

3. Do you consider Jesus to be your king? What is holding you back from experiencing the authentic love of Jesus Christ?

4. How can you better express compassion and charity to your family and those you might struggle with?

6

LET GO OF CONTROL: GROW IN MEEKNESS AND HUMILITY

The things that immediately concern the glory of God are very different from those of the world, for which much activity is necessary; as regards the things of God, we must be content to follow His inspirations and leave grace to act, cooperating wholeheartedly with its movements.

—St. Margaret Mary[1]

Trials Bring Opportunity

Prayer changes us from the inside out. When we are dealing with a problematic situation, pain, or suffering, it is an opportunity for us to grow in humility and become more like Christ by surrendering our own will and giving God control of our lives.

No one has an easy life; we all have moments of shame, pain, and difficulties, and the Lord wants to cleanse us and transform us into a new vessel so that we can share his love with others. Life's difficulties are opportunities for us to be purified and strengthened. Often in these moments of dire need, we can cling to our faith in a new way, and this can lead to a spiritual awakening that sets us back on the right path. Illness, diagnoses, and difficulties such as tragic accidents or unemployment can cause us to become bitter and angry—or to draw closer to Christ.

The love of the Sacred Heart can transform our hearts from the inside out, but we must be humble enough to ask for Jesus's love to be poured into us so that we can grow in holiness and find meaning and purpose in all we do and experience as sons and daughters of God. It is in the Sacred Heart that we come to understand our value.

As we will find in this next testimony, God hears our prayers and knows the desires of our hearts.

TESTIMONY FROM A HUMBLED HEART

I was professionally and personally on top of the world. Everything was moving in a positive direction, and it seemed like nothing could stop the momentum that was building . . . until something did. I had been bruising easily for a few weeks, and I noticed that those bruises weren't healing quickly. When I was at an event and found dark bruises up and down both legs, I went to the emergency room to have things checked out. They ran some blood tests, and in July I was diagnosed with an immune disorder called idiopathic thrombocytopenic purpura (ITP). This is a blood disease where your white blood cells go into overdrive and attack everything—particularly red blood cells.

The seriousness of the diagnosis was made clear to me as I was leaving the doctor's office, when a nurse ran out of the emergency room and stopped me in the parking lot, telling me I had to be admitted to the hospital immediately—she wouldn't even let me go home to gather my stuff. Typical red blood counts for an individual are around the twenty thousand mark—and my count (from the tests they ran) was two. I was told that if I were to fall and scrape my knee or cut myself shaving (or brushing teeth), I could bleed out.

I was admitted to the hospital, and eventually it was decided that I needed infusions (similar to chemotherapy) to bring my counts back to normal. During my third visit to the cancer center, God presented himself very clearly to me as I sat in a chair for six hours while they pumped a drug into me to make me sleep and then filled me with various steroids and chemicals to cure me. I had my laptop with me to work until I fell asleep, and on this particular day I was feeling pretty sorry for myself—and pretty angry at my situation.

I sat in the lounger. They punched the first IV into my arm and started the drip. As I took out my laptop, I looked up, frustrated, and said, "You suck," just to reiterate my point to God that I was very upset and angry about what he did to me. As if in response, a Sacred Heart of Jesus prayer card fell out of the laptop case and onto the little work table in front of me. But not the image side—the text side. And the first thing I read was the section of the prayer that said, "Make me humble, patient, pure, and wholly obedient to your will."

The previous spring, my beautiful wife and I had enthroned the Sacred Heart of Jesus in our home. Every day since then, I had prayed the Prayer of the Sacred Heart . . . and at that moment in that chair, I realized God had answered my prayers: an immune disorder is a very humbling disease. He made me patient; these treatments would continue for six months, and I would have to have checkups and tests for the rest of my life. He made me pure; these treatments were resetting my body and purifying my blood. The only thing left was to become wholly obedient to his will . . . and that day— that lesson—was the start of that journey.

I realized all of that at that moment. And just then, a frail stage 4 cancer patient walked in front of my chair— bald head covered in a bandana and walking slowly and deliberately toward her treatment. She looked at me, smiled, and said, "Good morning. Isn't it a wonderful day? God is good!" I shut my laptop, looked up, and quietly said, "Okay. I get it."

—A Man Whose Prayers Were Answered

PRAYING THROUGH OUR INNER STRUGGLES

The above testimony shows how God uses all things to bring about his glory. He uses our day's joys, works, and sorrows to teach us, instruct us, speak to our hearts, and form our minds. The Lord desires to humble us, not to crush us, for when we are humbled and open to him, he can rebuild us to be the very vessels of his eternal love and life.

The Bible says, "So humble yourselves under the mighty hand of God, that he may exalt you in due time" (1 Pt 5:6). St. Margaret Mary wrote, "Let us then submit to the orders of our sovereign Lord and, in spite of all that seems complicated and painful, let us confess that He is good and just in all that He does, and that He deserves to be honored and loved at all times."[2] When we are in the midst of the storms of life, we lack the clarity to see the hand of God at work. Each day we can experience real-life lessons that help us gain this clarity and perspective to better embrace the kingdom of God in our lives.

Imagine how impactful it must have been for this patient to go from anger at what the Lord had "taken away" to the illumination of seeing the stage 4 cancer patient giving God the glory despite her suffering. Suffering can be a mysterious catalyst for our conversion. No matter what the nature of that suffering might be—chronic or sudden, slight or serious, physical or spiritual—God can use it to expand our worldview and perspective. If we choose, it can be the impetus for inner transformation and lead us to lean on and trust in God in new and precious ways.

So why is it that suffering causes some to become bitter and others to go deeper in the faith? The key is whether we are open to building our relationship with our loving God. If we don't believe that God is loving, we can easily be tossed about by the sorrows and struggles of life and miss the beauty that fills our days. Grounding ourselves in the fundamental truth of God's love for us helps to protect our minds and hearts during difficult trials and tribulations.

The Old Testament speaks of the faithfulness of God and his love for humanity. He longs for us to take complete shelter in his loving heart by trusting in his ways even in difficult and painful times. The Bible tells us that "the LORD is good to those who wait for him, / a refuge on the day of distress, / Taking care of those who look to him for protection" (Na 1:7). Jesus shows us the path to heaven. And one of the most important ways we ready ourselves for heaven is through prayer. Prayer sustains us, keeping us always close to the prompting of the Holy Spirit and ever mindful of what we are missing in our day-to-day life. St. John Paul II wrote that prayer "is the secret of a truly vital Christianity."[3]

Jesus wants to cultivate a love relationship with our hearts, so that we learn to trust in his ways and to share that love with others. He wants to use the messiness of our lives to change, heal, and transform us. When we hit a low point and finally get on our knees and ask God to help us, we open the crack in the door of our hearts for him to come in. When our marriages are struggling, our finances are uncertain, our children are rebelling, or we or our family members are sick, this might be the very moment we are willing to get on our knees and turn it over to God. The problem for many in our society is that without knowledge of who God is, we can turn to bitterness and anger instead of prayer, which leads to peace and holiness.

How we respond to the difficult moments of life can be a powerful litmus test of where we are in our faith journey. We might check in with God at Mass when life is great, when life's trials are more trivial, but when our struggles take on a life-and-death seriousness or a complexity that requires us to rely on Christ for strength, we often turn to prayer as our last resort when in fact it is our most significant advantage. St. Josemaría wrote, "Prayer today is the only weapon, the most powerful means, for winning the battles of our interior struggles."[4]

So, how are we to win those interior battles?

1. *Know that you are at war with evil.* The devil desires to steal our joy and peace and to distract us from our end goal, which is salvation with God. These inner struggles can be as simple as learning to trust in the Lord, working on growing in virtue when a situation is challenging, or accepting the will of God even when it is difficult.

2. *Maintain a posture of humility and gratitude in order to receive from God what you need to win these spiritual*

battles. When we appreciate the joy-filled moments of life like young children, it becomes easier to live an abundant life here on earth. We won't get consumed by the pride and prestige of this world because we anticipate the joyful bounty of the next life. True humility leads to greatness, as the more we detach from pride, the closer we can become to God and enjoying life to the fullest.

3. *Be willing to see yourself as God sees you.* We must look beyond prestige, wealth, success, and flattery and arrive at the rawness of who we are. When we acknowledge our weaknesses and turn to the sacraments for restoration and renewal, our souls become like rich soil where the seeds of virtue we receive at baptism are watered and grow strong.

MEEKNESS AND HUMILITY: TRANSFORMATIVE VIRTUES THAT FLOW FROM THE HEART OF JESUS

"Meek, not weak" is a phrase I have found very helpful, as I serve in many leadership roles. I think Jesus clearly spelled out the virtues of his heart so that we could never be confused about how important meekness and humility are if we want to be like him: "Come to me, all you who labor and are burdened, and I will give you rest. Take my yoke upon you and learn from me, for I am meek and humble of heart; and you will find rest for yourselves. For my yoke is easy, and my burden light" (Mt 11:28–30).

It is easy and even tempting to overlook this holy habit, which the world ignores, maybe because meekness and humility aren't flashy and self-seeking. However, I can strongly argue that meek and humble people can leave a lasting and lifelong impression.

For example, we can think of St. Teresa of Calcutta and other saints and holy individuals who allowed Christ to change their hearts and could do even greater good without needing the world's affirmation. Their meekness and humility were refreshing and served as protection from the distraction of seeking fame and glory. When we strive to be meek and humble, we can do great things for Christ but remain unaware of and unshaken by the world.

In the holy scripture, Jesus tells us his heart is meek and humble. The opposite of meekness is arrogance and presumption, and the opposite of humility is pride. These sins block us from seeing God, encountering his heart, and being transformed by his ways. When we want to change, we need to do interior searching on how these vices have entered our souls and prevented us from seeing God. Pride is deadly because it numbs the heart to see life only from our limited perspective.

Think of a time when your pride prevented you from seeking forgiveness for some wrong you had done. It is like putting your heels deep in the sand as a way not to budge even if you are in the wrong! We must constantly seek the heart of Christ and evaluate whether we are meek and humble like the Lord so that he can use us. What better way to obtain heaven than to use meekness and humility as a road map to holiness? As Jesus said in Matthew 23:12, "Whoever exalts himself will be humbled; but whoever humbles himself will be exalted."

Enter the School of the Sacred Heart: Make Reparation

One of the most important ways our vices are weeded out to make room for virtue is through the struggles and pains of daily life. Think of the trials and hardships you have faced most recently—and how you responded. Did you turn bitter, or did you allow God to make you better? The great news is that it is never too late to ask the Lord to turn suffering into joy, or pain and sorrow into purposeful means of transformation. When we offer up our daily trials as acts of mortification, the Lord is able to work deeply in our lives, transforming us from the inside out.

We make reparation when we console Christ in his suffering, particularly the suffering caused by man's ingratitude, and give satisfaction for the outrages heaped upon Christ by our own sins and those of others.

In life we can choose to embrace our struggles and see the value in offering them back to Jesus, for he can bring good out of them. This isn't about ignoring our pains and suffering but rather about giving them back to God. Oftentimes we don't need to look far to find things to offer up. It might be a bad back, our daily chores and duties, or even a situation we find frustrating and difficult, like a broken appliance. Offering up these difficulties has value. Even more, we can offer up our prayers and offer Holy Communion back to Christ as a way to show him how much we love him.

In letters to her spiritual director Fr. Croiset, St. Margaret Mary tells us that this reparation is made precisely to the sanctity of love, and particularly for the lack of love shown to Jesus in the sacrament of his love. "Jesus asked to have a feast instituted to honor His Heart, and to make reparation for the ingratitude, irreverences and sacrileges men show to Him in the Sacrament of His love."[5]

In the Gospel of Luke, Jesus speaks about how we are to follow him: "If anyone wishes to come after me, he must deny himself and take up his cross daily and follow me" (Lk 9:23). Denying ourselves is learning to let go of our self-centered desires and tendencies and to let the Lord be our primary focus. As we continually spend time with Jesus in the Blessed Sacrament and also coming to learn how to unite our lives with his, we can experience even the painful moments of our lives with greater clarity, faith, and joy.

LET US PRAY:
PRAYER OF ST. MARGARET MARY

My Savior, I cheerfully accept all the painful dispositions, in which it is Thy pleasure to place me. My wish is in all things to conform myself to Thy

holy will. Whenever I kiss Thy cross, it is to show
that I submit perfectly to mine. Amen.[6]

REFLECTION QUESTIONS

1. How can meekness and humility help you grow closer
   to Jesus—and to other people?
2. Can you think of a time when your pride prevented
   you from reconciling with someone in your life? Ask
   the Sacred Heart to work in your heart, to give you the
   courage to take the next step to healing.
3. Have you ever experienced a hardship or trial so great
   that the burden seemed too much to bear? Might you
   be willing to offer it to Jesus to make reparation for sin?
   Can you ask him to give you the courage to make that
   sacrifice?
4. Have you spent much time contemplating pain caused
   to Jesus by man's ingratitude and coldness toward the
   Holy Eucharist? What can we do to better honor and
   show our love for the Lord?

1

PUT JESUS IN YOUR RELATIONSHIPS: THE GIFT OF FORGIVENESS

While at prayer, I begged our Lord to make known to me by what means I could satisfy the desire that I have to love Him. He gave me to understand, that one cannot better show one's love for Him than by loving one's neighbor for the love of Him; and that I must work for the salvation of others, forgetting my own interests in order to espouse those of my neighbor, both in prayers and in all the good I might be able to do by the mercy of God.

—St. Margaret Mary[1]

Love God, Love Others

Loving others is one of the most important tasks we can do here on earth. As we contemplate the life of Christ, we discover that our mission is to learn to love God and to love and serve others. We do not live in a "holy silo," isolated from the rest of the world; rather, we must work out our salvation by loving Christ through loving and forgiving others, including especially our family members.

Through the Sacred Heart devotion, the Lord invites us to be charitable and forgiving and to love those he places in our lives. Our witness to others is not only an opportunity to be the hands and feet of Christ to them, but also a powerful way to express compassion and forgiveness for their faults and failings and ask them to return that forgiveness to us when we offend and are hurtful. Here is one parent's story of embracing forgiveness through the Sacred Heart of Jesus.

TESTIMONY FROM A HEALED HEART

I couldn't let it go. I felt like I was holding a brick of unforgiveness that was heavy and was weighing me down. I found myself lashing out in anger, and my heart felt hard. Marriage and family life can be challenging even on a good day, but enduring the pain of a child letting you down by making potentially devastating decisions can be heart-wrenching.

I wanted to forgive and be a better person. And yet despite going to Confession to let go of the anger and hurt and to acknowledge the areas I could have done better, I still needed healing and a spiritual heart transplant. Then a dear friend encouraged me to begin the healing process by allowing the love of Christ to flow into my heart through forgiveness. Through the Sacred

Heart, I felt the fortress of my heart begin to open up, and I could ask God for the grace to forgive. I knew it would take time for my heart to heal and for our relationship to recover. The situation was complicated, yet my heart was the more significant issue at hand.

A few weeks after the incident, I was listening to praise music on the treadmill and began to reflect on my heart and the pain it was feeling from this family situation and the impact it would have on all of us. As I began to break a sweat during my morning run, I started to allow my mind to reflect on Jesus and when he died on the Cross.

Jesus was betrayed, disappointed, abandoned by his closest friends, and even insulted; a sword pierced his heart after he died. He was stretched out, his arms on the Cross, exposing himself even unto death. As I thought about that, I felt like Jesus said to my heart, "Where is your heart?" I didn't want to acknowledge how hurt it was, how pain-stricken it felt. I was still in a place of self-pity and anger. And yet I realized at that moment that just as Jesus exposed his heart to St. Margaret Mary, he was inviting me to do the same. He was asking me to "lift up my heart to the Lord" to be healed.

In my mind's eye, I saw my heart covered in thorns that only Jesus, the great physician and healer of all, could pull out! He reminded me that the crown of thorns circled his heart, and each thorn he pulled out of my heart, he tossed into the flame of his heart. As the lyrics of the song I was listening to at the time penetrated my heart, I realized that Jesus wanted to "be the king of my heart." I cried as I saw how much the Lord's heart is full of love and desires to heal us to set us free to live out the Gospel better. I was able to see that I was being invited to be compassionate and forgiving, and to help my child through showing him love and mentoring and not being resentful and pulling away. The healing that flooded my heart was an opportunity for a new beginning in our family.

—A Broken-Hearted Parent

THE WOUNDED HEART OF JESUS HEALS

This testimony is a powerful example of how the Lord desires to set us free from our burdens. He wants to show us what it means to love unconditionally and without expectations. How often do our expectations of our children, spouse, and other loved ones get in the way of truly loving them where they are, and then we end up feeling hurt and burdened? Only Jesus can remove the thorns and pains in our hearts, and only Jesus can show us the path forward. Without the love of Christ, we miss out on the transformation that can occur through learning to see the good in the other person and expressing forgiveness.

Jesus told us that the first commandment is "'You shall love the Lord your God with all your heart, with all your soul, with all your mind, and with all your strength.' The second is this: 'You shall love your neighbor as yourself.' There is no other commandment greater than these" (Mk

12:30–31). St. Margaret Mary wrote, "We must love Him with all our might and strength, no matter what it costs."[2]

The Lord wants to heal all of our hearts from the pains and sorrows of day-to-day life. No one is perfect; we will all be let down and hurt, but how we deal with it is what matters. The Most Sacred Heart of Jesus continually invites us to contemplate his love so that our hearts can be softened and "reset" to love the way he always intended.

According to St. Margaret Mary, "The Sacred Heart of Jesus is a burning furnace in which our hearts, so cowardly and cold, so faulty and imperfect, are tried and purified as gold in a crucible, in order that they be offered to Him as living victims, wholly immolated and sacrificed to His adorable designs."[3] Through his wounded heart, we are healed.

Fr. Mateo wrote, "How beautiful it is to think his heart beats in unison with ours. He loves as we love, all things good and lawful."[4] Jesus's most beautiful heart is the source of all grace, virtue, and healing. His heart beats out of love for us and, with that beating, desires to pump new life into our hearts and heal the areas that need new graces and healing.

Make Your Home More Loving through Forgiveness

One of the fastest ways to experience the love of the Sacred Heart and make this devotion your legacy is to stress the importance of the holy habit of forgiveness in your home. When we hurt others or are hurt by them, we need to go together to Jesus to find healing. We must ask the Sacred Heart to transform our weak hearts in the crucible of life so that we can share his forgiveness with others. And when we endure the tribulations of struggle and pain, we are invited to receive sweet graces from Christ that make us new through him.

Often we are tempted to hold out, to demand that the other person apologize before we forgive them. And yet it is never too soon to turn to the Sacred Heart and ask for the graces we need to forgive. Consider praying the Our Father and forgiving all those who have hurt you—even if they never apologize to you.

For some of us, it is challenging to say, "I am sorry." We think of a million reasons why apologizing is unnecessary—something to be forgotten, avoided, or smoothed over. But if we want to experience the true freedom of living with Christ at the center of our lives, we must be willing to remove anything that is preventing us from receiving those graces. Simply acknowledging our need to forgive or seek the forgiveness of others is not enough; it is like sitting down for a fancy meal and refusing the juicy steak—contenting ourselves with the decorative salad with a few sprigs of lettuce or a small potato. The meal would not be complete without what was intended to be in the center of the plate—the large steak. In the same way, when we avoid apologizing, we miss out on experiencing the peace of Christ within our hearts and extending that liberating freedom of the Gospel to others.

But what if someone has done something truly terrible, something you find impossible to forgive? What if a relationship has been so damaged that reconciliation is impossible? Bring it to the Sacred Heart, and ask Jesus to show you where to begin the work of mercy—the same mercy that allowed Jesus to forgive even those who killed him. Even if the person has died or we have serious reasons not to have this person in our lives, the goal is to keep our hearts free from sin and not to allow bitterness to develop. This bitterness is like a dark cloud that changes how we view ourselves and others. But when we turn toward the Sacred Heart and give Jesus room, the seeds of compassion begin to grow, producing a healing balm of forgiveness in our own hearts.

Jesus is inviting us not to place limits on how many times we forgive, just as God does not place limits on how often he forgives us. Each time we lift our hearts to the Lord to extend forgiveness, we exercise this spiritual muscle so that we become accustomed to "heavy lifting," causing less stress or strain the next time we extend God's forgiveness to others. Our fundamental goal is to learn not to be upset over trivial matters and to keep the joy, peace, and love of the Gospel in our hearts.

When complex and delicate matters need the balm of forgiveness, dig deep and unite those intentions with the power-packed virtue of charity. This will allow good to follow. We read in Romans 12:21, "Do not be conquered by evil but conquer evil with good."

FORGIVENESS: A POWERFUL VIRTUE THAT FLOWS FROM THE HEART OF JESUS

Unforgiveness can be a significant roadblock in family relationships and a place where evil can sneak in and take root like a cancer. When loved ones stop talking, interacting, and relating, eventually the family unit starts to crumble away. This disease can impact any relationship, from parent-child relationships, to those between siblings, to those with more distant relatives, and even to friendships. Without the hope and healing of Jesus, darkness prevails. When we choose not to cultivate hearts like the Lord's, we miss out on the graces of healing and hope.

When our hearts hurt, we hurt. Yet Jesus's heart is the most wounded and afflicted heart: Friends and loved ones abandoned him, he was humiliated, and the very people who had worshiped him days before chanted for his death. Lastly, Jesus's human heart, which contained divine love, was pierced with a lance after he died. But Jesus invites us to experience radical healing through that loving and wounded heart. We are invited to love him with all our strength no matter what the cost and no matter how we might feel in the moment. The Lord is teaching each of us life lessons, giving us the opportunity to grow spiritually through our response to the ups and downs of life. When we allow our hurt and pain to get in the way of loving God and others, it dramatically decreases our ability to love like Christ.

No matter what has hurt your heart, it needs to experience the love and graces that flow from Jesus. In the society we live in, it seems rare for someone to directly seek forgiveness. Instead of "I'm sorry I did this," you might hear instead "I am sorry you feel that way." In other words, "I am sorry you are sad" rather than "I am sorry I hurt you." And yet when we don't claim our wrongs and move forward, we keep the pain, hurt, and brokenness in our soul's darkness. It is like being trapped in a back storage room instead of being brought into the light.

Jesus is inviting us to be powerful witnesses to his love and mercy through giving and receiving forgiveness. The *Catechism* reminds us that we are asked to forgive others as Christ has forgiven us: "It is not in our power not to feel or to forget an offense; but the heart that offers itself to the Holy Spirit turns injury into compassion and purifies the memory in transforming the hurt into intercession" (*CCC*, 2843).

Forgiveness is not about a feeling but rather about a decision to let go so your heart is free to love God better. Recall the words of Jesus: "When you stand to pray, forgive anyone against whom you have a grievance, so that your heavenly Father may in turn forgive you your transgressions" (Mk 11:25).

As we contemplate the Sacred Heart, Jesus invites us to have faith, to trust in him, and to believe that God can use all things for his glory. St. Paul wrote, "We know that all things work for good for those who love God, who are called according to his purpose" (Rom 8:28). This scripture speaks to the wonder of God—that he will use the hurts, sufferings, and "blows" of life to bring a greater glory out of them.

When we allow our emotions to control our lives and rationalize our resistance to forgiving someone who has hurt us, we become "stuck," spiritually speaking. We cannot move forward and create new paths for the Lord to work in us. Jesus is always inviting us to forgive so that our hearts can be softened; through forgiving others, we gain a better scope on our own sinfulness and the need to acknowledge our faults.

Forgiveness begins with a special grace that expands the heart, so we can forgive without limit. St. John Chrysostom wrote, "Nothing makes us so like God, as being ready to forgive."[5] How we live and how we forgive are closely linked. Forgiveness is a lifestyle that allows us to be set free from the past; the devil cannot chain us to unforgiveness so long as our hearts are open and welcoming to the Sacred Heart of Christ. Jesus doesn't want us to cling to our hurt and pain; he wants to teach us how to let him rule our hearts with his love and healing graces.

This doesn't mean that others will not hurt us; instead, we will know what to do with the hurt and pain we experience in our lives and, through our suffering, we will be better able to love Christ and others.

ENTER THE SCHOOL OF THE SACRED HEART: THE GIFT OF CONFESSION

Besides living out devotion to the Sacred Heart, we are also continuously invited to attend Confession regularly to be set free from our sins and gain new graces. The Church teaches us to receive this sacrament at least once a year, before Easter. If you are struggling to forgive someone—or to be reconciled with someone you have harmed—sacramental Confession can be a beautiful way to take that first step toward freedom.

The final words exchanged in Confession are powerful and freeing. The priest ends the Confession with, "Your sins are forgiven. Go in peace." And we are invited to say, "Thanks be to God." I recall a few specific Confessions in my life where I have said these final words with a spirit of total relief and joy. After Confession, we are able to move forward to better live out our Christian walk and vocation. At times, I have even thanked the priest for his vocation, and I have found myself offering prayers of gratitude for this Sacrament of Healing. The Lord wants to free us from sin and strengthen us to live our faith better.

Reconciliation is a gift to wash the soul and start fresh! Here is a prayer you can use to help you prepare for your next encounter with Jesus in the Sacrament of Reconciliation.

LET US PRAY:
PRAYER FOR HELP TO FORGIVE

Lord Jesus,

My heart feels like an impenetrable stone as I am struggling to forgive _____. Please trade my hardened heart for one that flows with your mercy. Give me the grace to let go of bitterness, a desire for revenge, and the need for an apology. Set me free from the captivity of my unforgiving heart and fill me with your healing love. Amen.[6]

REFLECTION QUESTIONS

1. As you ponder the image of the Sacred Heart and think about those you most need to forgive and receive forgiveness from, which names come to mind? Talk to Jesus about them.
2. What is preventing you from truly forgiving this person—whether or not this person is still in your life?
3. How can you be a better witness in being a person who seeks to forgive? When we take the time to acknowledge our pain and our hurts and seek to forgive, we are more like Christ.

4. What can you let go of? What do you need to get better at forgiving and forgetting so that you don't harbor bitterness?

8

BREAK ATTACHMENTS AND ADDICTIONS: THE POWER OF TEMPERANCE AND SELF-CONTROL

Publish this devotion everywhere, propagate it, recommend it to people of the world as a sure and easy means to obtain from Me a true love for God; . . . as an assured means to touch the hardest of hearts; and finally to all the faithful, as a most solid devotion, and one most proper to obtain victory over the strongest passions, to establish union and peace in the most divided families; to get rid of the most long-standing imperfections; to obtain a most ardent and tender love for Me; in short, in fine, to arrive in little time and in a very easy manner, at the most sublime perfection.

—Jesus to St. Margaret Mary[1]

IS SOMETHING OUT OF ORDER IN YOUR LIFE?

The words that Jesus shared with St. Margaret Mary remind us that Christ wants to help us in all areas of our lives. When we are in the midst of a dark time, it is hard to imagine how the Lord can set us free from our addictions and attachments. Instead of us having a grip on them, they have a stranglehold on us.[2]

The Most Sacred Heart of Jesus promises that he will help us control the passions and forces that bind us. The first step to this long-term transformation is allowing the love of Christ into our hearts and seeing that Jesus desires to set up his kingdom in our hearts and souls. God does not want our disordered behaviors and passions to mislead us; instead, he wants to help us overcome them. The Sacred Heart is the source of hope and strength we need to break away from these destructive behaviors.

When we are suffering and chained to sin and sinful lifestyles, Jesus invites us to let him into those dark corners of our lives. The only way to let go and let God is through a deep and personal transformation such that the old ways are no longer our ways.

When we are in times of trouble or the "low place" in life, the world offers numbing solutions to the soul such as alcohol, pain pills, pornography, and emotional distancing. These solutions lead to more pain. Jesus has something better: He wants to transform homes through spiritual protection. He wants to strengthen us when we fight our "demons" that draw us into sin and addiction.

Listen to these words of St. Margaret Mary: "Since it is not the divine good pleasure to still the tempest within you, I beg the Sacred Heart to be Himself your support, so that you may remain firm, immovable, and tranquil in the midst of the storm, which must not disturb you at all, for it cannot overpower you."[3]

Here is a testimony from someone moved by the love of Jesus in the Sacred Heart to choose family and health over alcohol.

TESTIMONY FROM A SOBER HEART

I am grateful to the Most Sacred Heart of Jesus. I feel like as I grew closer to him, Jesus convinced me that my drinking was hurting me and my family. I saw how I was not choosing my God, my family, and my mental health with each drink, but rather allowing my excessive drinking to dictate my life. I am so thankful for the deep and personal love of the Sacred Heart to help sustain my sobriety. Now, I can see that God desires to offer me much more than I ever gained from drinking. Slowly I am learning that I need to learn to grow more dependent on him and live in the present moment.

—A Grateful Catholic

THE ANGEL OF ALCOHOLICS ANONYMOUS

The courage that flows from the heart of Jesus helps us believe that the Lord is offering us "the abundant life," a lifestyle based on the freedom to love and serve God. Addiction and disordered attachments prevent us from living a life wholly committed and devoted to him.

One powerful example of how the Sacred Heart of Jesus inspired a tremendous movement of healing and hope for addicts worldwide is the story of a simple nun named Sr. Mary Ignatia (1889–1966), the "Angel of Alcoholics Anonymous," who ministered in Akron, Ohio. She wore a white habit and dedicated her life to helping alcoholics get the help they needed to experience freedom from their addiction. This Sister of Charity of Saint Augustine befriended the founders of Alcoholics Anonymous (AA), Dr. Robert Smith ("Dr. Bob") and Bill Wilson. She met Dr. Bob in 1930 at St. Thomas Hospital in Akron, Ohio, and later worked at St. Vincent Charity Hospital in Cleveland. She contributed to the organization by highlighting the importance of the spiritual aspect to overcoming addiction and showing the men compassion and kindness. Sr. Ignatia worked the admission desk and is credited with admitting the first "drunk" to the hospital under another diagnosis issued by Dr. Smith to get the man the help he needed, despite the policy of not accepting drunks. That day, August 16, 1935, marked the beginning of Alcoholics Anonymous.

Sr. Ignatia was a significant spiritual leader in the early years of the AA movement. She had a strong understanding of the importance of sobriety and, in the early stages of this life-changing ministry, invested her whole life in helping alcoholics. Her spirituality as a religious sister brought much clarity and formation to the men who would come to the ward at St. Thomas Hospital for help. She would counsel the addicts, "Just tell him in your own words that you have made a mess of your life, and ask him if he won't take over from here. . . . Just tell him that you are going to put your life in his hands, and have the serenity to accept his holy will and all that he sends."[4] In this way, she inspired her patients to accept both what they could change—their drinking habits—and what they could not—their ongoing addiction.

Sr. Ignatia would encourage patients to ask the Lord to supply them with the wisdom they needed to remain sober and to restore many of their broken relationships. She encouraged the patients to "treat God as if he were a friend, worthy of their secrets and anxious for their company." When they were ready, this little Sister would lead the men to the chapel and "gently show each embarrassed, doubtful man how to bend his knees and pray. Tough men lost their pride and knelt down on the floor beside her. Many said they found God this way."[5]

Not only did this special Sister give compassion, kindness, and loving instruction to these men, but she desired to introduce them to Jesus Christ. When they were discharged, she would hand each of them two things: a copy of *The Imitation of Christ*, by Thomas à Kempis, and a Sacred Heart medal. She would tell them that if they decided to take a drink, they would have to return the little medallion to her at the desk. Handing these patients the image of the Sacred Heart was a tangible sign that she was placing their addiction into the care of the Sacred Heart. It is said that many of these men kept these medallions in their wallets and thanked God for this loving and kind Sister who led them to Christ and to sobriety.

Although the medals were later replaced by the tokens members receive today to mark the milestones of their sobriety, Sr. Ignatia is credited with establishing another practice associated with AA—the coffee bar, which she established in the "Rosary Hall Solarium" at St. Vincent's Charity Hospital after Dr. Bob's death in 1952. To this day, Sr. Ignatia is credited with the constant flow of fresh coffee at every Twelve-Step meeting. This humble and straightforward nun made a world of difference in the lives of so many.

COPING WITH AND ACCOMPANYING THOSE WITH ADDICTIONS

Sr. Ignatia is a powerful example of using faith to transform lives. She not only shared the Gospel with these men struggling to break free from their addiction, but she showed them through her attention and service how much she cared for them. In the same way, we must continue to love and safeguard the dignity of those caught in the chains of addiction and their toxic habits that are sadly hurting and impeding their relationships with those they care most about. With God's help, we can prayerfully accompany those seeking to overcome addiction, asking the Sacred Heart to pour grace into their hearts so that they might experience a far more rewarding life. She might have known the promise our Lord gave St. Margaret Mary when he said, "He promised to pour out into the hearts of all those who honor the image of His Heart all the gifts which It contains. He promised also to imprint His love on the hearts of all those who would wear this image on their persons, and that He would destroy in them all disordered movements."[6] As Catholics, we can see that Jesus longs to strengthen, help, and heal us.

The Lord is such a good and gentle God; he will never ask beyond our ability to give. Whether it is our own addiction or that of a beloved family member or friend, he invites us to surrender out-of-control passions and desires and replace them with virtues and even alternatives to destructive behaviors like giving up drinking and drugs. When we encounter the love of Christ and learn to lean on him, we can experience profound freedom as we surrender these destructive behaviors to God. This new way of thinking and behaving can transform patterns for living and even save lives. For example, Sr. Ignatia knew that coffee was an excellent replacement for a drink of alcohol. Jesus is a good and gentle God who works with our humanity in a way that strengthens us. So often we think we are giving up our "fun," and then God shows us instead that we were imprisoned by what held us back.

I have been amazed at the number of families who have revealed that once they began to live out a Christ-centered life dedicated to the Sacred Heart, addiction and disorder became intolerable. What was once a way of living was now no longer acceptable. Our good God desires to set us free from what holds us down—from pornography, drugs, and alcohol. Addiction has no place when you want to live out a Christ-centered life. Jesus reveals our weaknesses so that he can heal us from the destructive behaviors that hold us back from living life abundantly.

Addiction and toxic habits are infiltrating families like never before. We are invited to give Jesus our total "yes" so that these destructive behaviors do not hold us back from experiencing his love. Sr. Margaret Mary wrote, "May the Sacred Heart accomplish in you all His designs and be Himself your strength and your stay, so as to enable you to bear courageously the weight of your responsibilities."[7]

Sometimes families caught up in the cycle of addiction hesitate to welcome Jesus into their home or worry that "something bad" will happen before the Enthronement of the Sacred Heart takes place. Don't let such worries prevent you from cultivating a more profound devotion to the heart of Jesus. Fr. Stash Dailey once said, "If you are afraid to welcome the Reign of Christ into your heart and home through the enthronement, then the devil is already winning." I have never known anyone to regret doing the enthronement; if anything, they have wished that they hadn't put it off or that they had sought to live out the devotion earlier in their lives.

Our spiritual journey, or lack thereof, has eternal consequences, leading us ever closer to heaven or hell. These two kingdoms are different destinations, contradicting endpoints. We can either invest in our relationship with God and cultivate the kingdom of God here on earth, seeking to love God and others, or we can spread hate, anger, and sin here on earth on our way to live forever with Satan. So when life is challenging, we need to pause and consider the long-term impact of our decisions and actions in light of eternity. Without faith, we can not only shipwreck our own lives but greatly injure our families as well.

If you feel overwhelmed by distractions, collect your thoughts in the tranquil depths of the Sacred Heart. Our Lord will infallibly give you the victory over these distractions, provided you fight vigorously against them.

TEMPERANCE: A VIRTUE OF SELF-CONTROL THAT FLOWS FROM THE HEART OF JESUS

With complicated matters like addiction, we need to pray for Jesus to flood us with the virtues of temperance and self-control so that we can better live out the will of God in our lives and avoid sin. If we feel surrounded and overwhelmed by impulsive decisions, these virtues will help us pause and recognize the impact of our life decisions on others.

When we ask the Lord to flood us with the virtue of temperance, we can better navigate the temptations that fill our lives with guardrails to help us live out our choices. The key to this virtue is to live it with joy in our hearts, knowing that we best serve the Lord when we practice this foundational virtue.

The holy habit of temperance is not just for those struggling with addiction but for everyone. We read in 1 Peter 5:8, "Be sober and vigilant. Your opponent the devil is prowling around like a roaring lion looking for [someone] to devour." The devil wants to tear us apart through destructive behaviors that hold us back from the abundant life. We can practice temperance not only with what we eat and drink but also with how we manage our technology, leisure, and even our life balance. When we flex the temperance muscle, we might get more sleep and live a better, healthier life!

In family life, our temperance might be someone else's prayer request. We can overcome peer pressure when we learn to say, "No, thank you," out of love for God. As our bodies are temples of the Holy Spirit, we are responsible for caring for and treating them with respect and kindness. When we embrace self-control, we come to appreciate the freedom it offers us, and it also helps to strengthen other virtues such as purity and even a sense of justice.

When we live out temperance and self-control, we are able to be powerful witnesses to a world where so many self-medicate through overindulging in substances that alter reality. Now is the time to be a holy witness to our sobriety and desire to grow in virtue.

Enter the School of the Sacred Heart: Night Adoration

For those living with watching a loved one experience disorder and pain from an addiction, night adoration in the home can be a sustaining, healing practice. The beautiful devotion of the holy hour became well-known and practiced in the United States in the 1950s, and many families have seen tremendous blessings. When family members offer a holy hour right in the home before the Sacred Heart image, their prayers of reparation out of love of Christ are powerful.

A holy hour can be as simple as praying before the image and uniting your heart with a Mass prayed around the world in another time zone, or something more formal such as praying a Rosary or Divine Mercy chaplet. This prayer time works best when we commit to prayer and ask the Lord to help our family members and us.

Fr. Mateo wrote, "How beautiful it is to think His heart beats in unison with ours. . . . He loved as we love, all things good and lawful. His Heart, 'yesterday, today, and the same forever,' never changes in its affection, its tenderness, its predilection."[8] Night adoration is a great way to pray to the Most Sacred Heart of Jesus and connect with his beautiful, beating heart.

Your holy hour at home is a small sacrifice in light of the pain and suffering of so many. Plan one each month, or make a spontaneous holy hour with the Lord instead of tossing and turning in bed at night. I have found that when I spend time at home in night prayer before my Sacred Heart image, I never miss the sleep; instead, I am thankful for those quiet moments in worship right in my home.

LET US PRAY: PRAYER FOR DAILY NEGLECTS

Eternal Father, I offer Thee the Sacred Heart of Jesus, with all its love, all its sufferings and all its merits.

First—To expiate all the sins I have committed this day and during all my life. [Glory Be.*]

Second—To purify the good I have done poorly this day and during all my life. [Glory Be.]

Third—To supply for the good I ought to have done, and that I have neglected this day and during all my life. [Glory Be.]9

*Glory Be to the Father, and to the Son, and to the Holy Spirit, as it was in the beginning, is now, and ever shall be, world without end. Amen.

REFLECTION QUESTIONS

1. Ask the Lord to reveal an addiction that has a grip on you or an area where you lack self-control, such as having a short temper or acting impulsively. How can the virtue of temperance help you?
2. How has addiction affected your life? Do you have a sensitivity to others going through this difficulty?
3. How can faith strengthen your walk through addiction?
4. What is the role of the virtues of temperance and self-control in your life?

9

EXPAND THE KINGDOM: PRACTICE JOY AND GRATITUDE

Above all, I beg you to be always gay [lighthearted and carefree], joyful and happy, for this is the true mark of the Spirit of God, Who wishes that we should serve Him in peace and contentment; do not be uneasy or anxious, but do all things with liberty of mind and in the presence of God.

—St. Margaret Mary[1]

A Simple Remedy for a Troubled Heart

These words of St. Margaret Mary remind us not to be anxious or uneasy, echoing the words of Jesus himself, who tells us often in the gospels, "Do not be afraid," and "Do not let your hearts be troubled." When we take time to allow the joy of the Gospel to set our hearts on fire and renew them, we can better love and serve others. Jesus wants to fill our lives with his grace and love and to be the king of our hearts. This holy habit of joy is one that will change not only your heart but your perspective on your life.

Just think of the joyful people you have encountered in your life. You desire to be around these people—they are calming, and it is almost as though the concerns of the world get washed away when you witness their peace and joy. Christians who take their "Christian joy" seriously and seek to spread the joy of Christ are potent witnesses, especially in family life.

We must be careful not to allow others to steal this joy and replace it with fear and anxiety. We quickly lose our peace and happiness by allowing modern media to stress us out and tempt us to worry about everything out of our control. How often do fear and anxiety cast a dark blanket of despair and darkness over us, especially when we can't solve the issue except by offering prayers and sacrifices to the Lord? When we allow the Gospel message to penetrate our hearts and focus on being more lighthearted and joyful, we can better love those around us and live prayerfully in the moment.

Just think of how little children can bring so much joy to a family. I can recall many times when my youngest's laughter or carefree spirit lightened the atmosphere and reminded us that "everything is going to be okay." When we allow the love of Christ to motivate us to express joy to others, we are better witnesses.

I also recall when my four- or five-year-old inquired, "When you answer the phone, why are you so happy and nice? But when you talk to us, you are cranky and forget to say please?" These words cut the core of my heart. I paused and realized that when someone I thought was important called, I would hush the kids, and in the rush of the moment, I could have done it with more kindness and consideration! I was the one who stole the joy of the moment with an unnecessary expectation. This was a powerful lesson for me to make sure to work on maintaining a disposition of peace and joy at home.

Here is the story of a mother of many who was inspired to live in gratitude and to love as God loves.

TESTIMONY FROM A GRATEFUL HEART

I held my baby in my arms, feeling overwhelmed at the sounds of the hustle and bustle of my life. Children were coming and going all around me, yet I felt like I was almost glued to my chair. I had just had another C-section, and my body felt tired from the inside out. I wasn't sure how I would get through one more day, much less many more years of parenting. As I sat there holding my youngest, I prayed and asked God for the grace to go forward, to love as he loves, and that he would help me.

As I looked lovingly at this beautiful newborn girl, I heard a small voice in my heart say, "But I love her so very much." With that, I shifted from fear to seeing the good and knowing our God loves each one of us like he loves this sweet little child. He loves my child; he loves me. He loves my family and the entire world. Since that moment, many years ago, I have tried to recall the importance of gratitude for every daily blessing, joy, and most of all the gift of life! I have embraced the importance of being grateful not only for my marriage and children but for everything, nature, my many daily blessings, and my faith.

—A Mother Growing in Gratitude

Embracing Our Everyday Life for Jesus

Motherhood and fatherhood require so much giving of self, yet I have found that if our love isn't rooted in God's love, we lack the well from which to draw love. God wants to pour his love upon us; he wants us to revel in that love and share it with others. St. Margaret Mary was blessed to see the heart of Christ; she wrote, "I hope your heart will become so inflamed with this love that it will transform you into Him and become one with His heart."[2] We are invited to experience that same unity with God through this life-changing devotion and the Blessed Sacrament. I look back and marvel over how God has touched my heart with his transformative love.

The more we embrace the joy of the Gospel and grow in gratitude, the more we shift away from judgment, resentment, and sin. This holy habit takes true training of the heart; we must be well aware that most people are not thinking this way, so they might not understand why we are the way we are. Our God is so good that the more we grow in gratitude, the more we will seek to not offend him through sin. This simple shift can make a difference as we seek to better honor the Most Sacred Heart of Jesus.

Jesus invites us to embrace our day-to-day life to better live out our Catholic faith. Our faith is not a rejection of the ordinary; rather, it turns everyday moments into extraordinary moments to obtain grace and be transformed. When we turn to Jesus in prayer and share both the good and the challenging moments in our lives, he is better able to equip us. I like to say to the Lord when I wake up, "What do you have in store for me today?" This question helps me to remember that every day is a gift and I have new experiences awaiting me.

Without the help of Christ, and without developing holy habits, it is easy to resent life's ordinary moments, which are actually our path to holiness. This sanctifying path might include getting up with young children at night, cleaning, cooking, working, or just living out life's simplest moments. The difference is not what we do but whether we are willing to allow these moments to produce grace through prayer.

One of the defining elements of our lives is our attitude and how we perceive our reality. When I was a young parent, the time went by so slowly that I would count down the hours waiting for my husband to come home. I was lonely and trying to adjust to motherhood. During these early years, I kept focusing on when my children would grow up rather than maximizing and appreciating each day. I almost wished those early years of being a mom away as I thought, "I will like it when they can walk and talk." My perspective shift of growing in the holy habit of gratitude led to a significant change in my attitude and how I filled my days. Instead of focusing on what I didn't have, a stage in life I wasn't in, or even what I was missing out on, I slowly embraced the moment at hand with a spirit of gratitude. I found that, over time, I was no longer struggling with wishing time away or waiting for others to fill my needs, but instead, I learned how the holy habit of gratitude could transform even the most mundane moments. I also began to surround myself with new friends who witnessed how to embrace this virtue better.

We are all invited to sanctify the ordinary moments of our lives through prayer and gratitude. When we fail to allow the love of Christ to warm our hearts, we quickly grow cold, hardhearted, and self-focused. Gratitude allows us to keep our eyes on God and to praise, worship, and thank him for our lives and all the moments that fill our days.

The Mass: Our Greatest Gift

If we want hearts transformed by the Sacred Heart, there is no more powerful way to welcome Jesus into our hearts than going to Mass, receiving Jesus in the Eucharist, and giving praise and glory for the Blessed Sacrament. Jesus is truly present in the Blessed Sacrament, and when we turn to him with our praise and adoration, we are better able to live a life of deep gratitude—and he is better able to work in our hearts.

According to Fr. Mateo, "From the altar He gently calls the poor, the sad, the outcast. From the depths of the Tabernacle He is ever stretching out His arms to those who are hungering for justice and for *love*."[3] Fr. Mateo is reminding us that we are invited to encounter Christ through receiving the Holy Eucharist, our spiritual food. St. Margaret Mary wrote, "Let every knee bend before Thee, O greatness of my God, so supremely humbled in the Sacred Host. May every heart love Thee, every spirit adore Thee, and every will be subject to Thee."[4]

The Sacred Heart of Jesus is the heart of the very same God present to us in the Blessed Sacrament. St. Margaret Mary shared that "Jesus makes Himself poor in the Blessed Sacrament; He gives us all He has, reserving nothing for Himself, so as to possess our hearts and enrich them with Himself. I must forsake and despise myself, if I wish to imitate Him and to win His most lovable Heart."[5] Jesus desires to give us spiritual food for our journey to heaven; why not take advantage of this nourishment?

We must guard against the cultural trend that encourages us to drift from the sacraments, including from attending Holy Mass; this leads to anorexia of the soul. The Holy Eucharist is our greatest gift here on earth, for in it we are invited to receive Jesus himself. The *Catechism* tells us that "the Eucharist is 'the source and summit of the Christian life' (*Lumen Gentium*, 11). 'The other sacraments, and indeed all ecclesiastical ministries and works of the apostolate, are bound up with the Eucharist and are oriented toward it. For in the blessed Eucharist is contained the whole spiritual good of the Church, namely Christ himself, our Pasch' (*Presbyterorum Ordinis*, 5)" (*CCC*, 1324).

The Eucharist is the center of our Catholic faith. When we come to believe that Jesus is truly present in the Eucharist, we can begin not only to appreciate this terrific gift but to worship the Lord in a new way. We can see the Eucharist as our spiritual food for our journey to heaven. If you desire a spiritual heart transplant, begin with encountering the Lord in the Blessed Sacrament. St. Margaret Mary once said, "As for your Communions, they must produce in you such good effects that you will no longer commit deliberate sins."[6]

What if we thought of receiving Holy Communion as a means to heal, strengthen, and help our souls? What if we saw it as the spiritual food we *need* to live? As Catholics, we can easily fall into the practice of not living our faith and just showing up out of habit. The Sacred Heart of Jesus is a visible reminder that his heart beats out of love for us and his Body and Blood are our food for our entire life journey.

GRATITUDE: A KINGDOM-BUILDING VIRTUE THAT FLOWS FROM THE HEART OF JESUS

Everything we have—our lives, our homes, our families, our jobs, and our vocations—is gifted to us from God. When we lose sight of this—when we wish away these blessings or become envious of the gifts God entrusts to others—we cannot see and experience the kingdom of God unfolding right in our lives. Fr. Mateo wrote, "Do you know the easiest way to final damnation? It is the path of ingratitude, the path taken by those who wrong a God of Love."[7]

The book *In Conversation with God* states that "thankfulness is a way of expressing our faith because we recognize God as the source of all good; it is the sign of hope because we accept that all good comes through him, and it leads to love and humility because we acknowledge our poverty and our need."[8] Learning to respond with gratitude is a way for us to better thank God for all he provides us and to build our trust in his ways. For God is a good God who desires to lead us to heaven. Part of our path to heaven might be challenging moments where he teaches us and instructs us like a parent with a young child. These moments are designed to lead us to take our eyes off ourselves and place them back on God.

St. Paul wrote, "In all circumstances give thanks, for this is the will of God for you in Christ Jesus" (1 Thes 5:18). For many of us, giving thanks is very difficult. We constantly grapple with how things "should have been."

While God promises not to provide us with more than we can handle, he does want us to become more dependent and focused on him; often these difficult times unite us with his heart and bring us to our knees.

Gratitude is essential for sharing the love that flows from the heart of Jesus: gratitude to God not only for everything in our lives but for his blessings to others as well. Words of gratitude—giving thanks first to God and then to other people for all the ways they bless our lives—are a powerful way to spread the love of Christ and allow this to be part of our legacy of love.

How often do little acts of ingratitude form in our hearts, impacting our perspective and ultimately leading to a sense of entitlement? By cultivating hearts of gratitude, we will remain acutely sensitive to all the graces and gifts God gives us. We need to reject the culture of ingratitude and help our children do the same. One action that has made an enormous difference in my life is to share a prayer of gratitude with my children on the way to school and to end the day with this same prayer thanking God for all his blessings. When we open our hearts to this holy habit and give Christ all the thanks, we find ingratitude less and less attractive.

ENTER THE SCHOOL OF THE SACRED HEART: FIRST FRIDAY DEVOTION

The Lord invites us to grow closer to him in the Holy Eucharist. St. Margaret Mary shared, "Let every knee bend before Thee, O greatness of my God, so supremely humbled in the Sacred Host. May every heart love Thee, every spirit adore Thee, and ever will be subject to Thee!"[9]

The Holy Eucharist is so central to the Sacred Heart devotion that Jesus instructed St. Margaret Mary about the importance of attending Mass and receiving Holy Communion on the First Friday of the month. This First Friday devotion is a reminder of the day Jesus died on the Cross and a way that our Holy Communion can be an act of reparation for our sins and the sins against Jesus in the Blessed Sacrament. Living out the First Friday devotion is an essential aspect of the Sacred Heart devotion. This is when we pause in our busy lives and go to Mass to recall the greatest sacrifice, the death of Jesus.

According to St. Margaret Mary, the First Friday devotion carries a powerful promise from Jesus: "On Friday during Holy Communion, He said these words to His unworthy slave, if I mistake not: 'I promise you in the excessive mercy of My Heart that Its all-powerful love will grant to all those who receive Holy Communion on nine first Fridays of consecutive months the grace of final repentance; they will not die under My displeasure or without receiving their sacraments, My divine Heart making Itself their assured refuge at the last moment.'"[10]

The greatest gift we can ever receive is to allow the Lord to enter our hearts. Msgr. John Esseff, a Roman Catholic priest from Pennsylvania, was ordained to the priesthood in 1953, served as the retreat director and

confessor to St. Mother Teresa and the Missionaries
of Charity, and was a spiritual mentor to St. Padre Pio.
When I asked him on the phone about the link between
the Sacred Heart and the Eucharist he recited: "Allow the
Holy Eucharist to explode within your soul. Each time
we receive the Body and Blood of Jesus Christ, we also
welcome his soul and divinity. We must recall that every
single good gift comes from the Lord. Allow the Holy
Eucharist to take on new meaning in your life because
of the love of Christ." He also shared a message he has
been preaching for years: "You are Christ in the world.
That's who you are. You are Jesus. Now go and be Jesus
to others."[11] This holy and kind priest has not only lived a
full life but even in his later years serves others on behalf
of the kingdom through living out a holy priesthood and
passing on the faith.

On one of the First Fridays this year, I had a full
schedule and was going to have to miss Mass. As I sat in
the school parking lot after dropping off the children, I
decided to rework my schedule and go to Mass instead of
doing what I had planned. Sitting in the church, I began
to reflect on the gift of this monthly "reset." What a blessing it is to have a mini Good Friday every First Friday, to
refocus my spiritual life back on Jesus.

As Mass began, I discovered that the intention of that
Mass was for the repose of the soul of my old neighbor,
who I didn't know had passed away. I felt a sense of comfort as I prayed for his soul and thought of the kind things

he had done for our young family, like giving us a bunch of Christmas lights, extra candy bars at Halloween, and always a warm hello when he saw us. During Holy Communion, I saw his wife, Judy, walk up the main aisle. I reached out to give her a small hug, and we both began tearing up. She was so happy to have me there at Mass, and I was so grateful I went. As I approached Holy Communion, I thanked God for this very special moment, which only happened because I said yes to going to Mass on the First Friday of the month. I believe I was meant to be there for my old neighbor and my sister in Christ.

Did you know that the word *Eucharist* is based on the Greek word meaning "thanksgiving"? For what are you most thankful today? Begin your day by praising the Lord and declaring what you are grateful for in your life. Share five things you are grateful for, and ask him to help you to see his loving hand throughout your day. When we train our eyes to see the Lord working, we can better love, serve, and honor him. In the evening, thank Jesus for specific things he did or provided for you this day. When we are grateful, we are able to be transformed by God and gain a whole new perspective on our lives.

LET US PRAY: ACT OF CONSECRATION TO THE SACRED HEART

My loving Jesus, out of the grateful Love I bear You, and to make reparation for my unfaithfulness to grace, I give You my heart, and I consecrate

myself wholly to You; and with Your help I purpose to sin no more. Amen.[12]

REFLECTION QUESTIONS

1. Can you recall a time when you struggled to be
   grateful?
2. How have you experienced the Eucharist as your spiritual food for the journey toward heaven?
3. What is a spiritual gift the Lord has provided you that
   you are most grateful for? Could it be a virtue, a grace,
   a charism of the spirit?
4. Have you heard of the First Friday devotion? Have you
   considered taking up this powerful spiritual practice?

LIVE IN THE KINGDOM OF PEACE: LET PRUDENCE GUIDE YOU

May the peace of the adorable Heart of Jesus Christ ever fill our hearts, so that nothing may be able to disturb our serenity!

—St. Margaret Mary[1]

Finding the Way of Peace

Jesus affirms that one of the most significant rewards of following him is the peace he offers us. He tells us in the gospels, "Peace I leave with you; my peace I give you. Not as the world gives it do I give it to you" (Jn 14:27). St. Paul wrote, "For he is our peace" (Eph 2:14). He is our medicine for the pain this world inflicts, a healing remedy made manifest through the peace we experience when we accept him into our hearts.

Sin causes a lack of inner peace and allows fear, sadness, and loneliness to take hold of us. Sin destroys our internal order, separates us from God, and robs us of the inner peace he intends for us. When we cut off our relationship with Christ and start to distrust and worry, we need to pause and put our concerns in perspective. Is this really worth worrying and being stressed about? This is why it is so essential that we seek Christ with our whole hearts and ask him to bestow peace in our souls. A tremendous little catchy phrase I love to recite is "I am too blessed to be stressed." The truth is Jesus doesn't want us to worry. Instead, he invites us to grow closer to him in prayer, divine trust, and striving to keep our inner peace despite what takes place around us.

The heart of Jesus desires to fill us with his lasting peace that will overcome any of our worst moments and keep us far away from sin and a sinful lifestyle. Many, once they begin to grow closer to Christ, find their sins less appealing, for the peace and joy of being a Christian outweighs temptation to sin. We can only have peace in our hearts when we ditch resentment and bitterness and embrace joy and peace. When we begin to resist the life tasks and challenges that God has given us each day in order that we may grow closer to him, resentment creeps in and robs us of our inner peace and joy. Resentful, negative emotions cause a dark fog to cover our lives and relationships, obscuring our intended path. Unless we remain close to the heart of Jesus, which acts like a lantern emanating rays of grace to light our path, we will lose our way.

When on a journey, we follow the twists and turns of the road made by the highway engineers because we trust that they intended our good and chose the way according to the dictates of the landscape to get us to our destination safely and in the most reasonably direct way. We don't stop to question every obstacle they faced or every boulder they had to remove to construct the road we are on. So too, we should not spend excessive energy questioning the path God has set before us. We can never fully comprehend God's ways; our task is to simply respond with love to what the Lord provides, especially the gifts and even the crosses of life.

Think of how difficult it is to do a task when you are resentful and have become angry and consumed by your thoughts, preventing you from having peace. I recall a time in childhood when I was so resentful and jealous of my siblings for getting out of cleaning that I could not think clearly. All I could think was "Why are they not here?" Even though they were helping in other ways by mowing the lawn, babysitting, or running errands for my parents, I allowed jealousy and resentment to destroy my inner peace, leaving me miserable. This small example reminds us how resentment and jealousy can not only lead us astray in our thoughts and feelings but break down relationships as well. When we focus our eyes on "self," we miss the opportunity to be like Jesus.

Offering frequent prayers to Jesus is a powerful holy habit that can help you grow closer to him. First, try small prayers like "Lord, fill my soul with your peace and joy," or "Jesus, I offer up these tasks I don't want to do, but I ask you to be with me." Knowing that you are not alone, that God is with you, makes it much easier to maintain your peace while serving him through the ordinary.

St. Margaret Mary shares in her letters to Mother de Saumaise, "This loving Heart, I assure you, is at present my whole occupation, not only during prayer but always. I find in It a paradise of peace which makes me indifferent to everything else. Everything else seems contemptible in comparison."[2] Just think, God is offering us also a "paradise of peace," a radical understanding of peace; that shouldn't be disturbed even in the midst of daily life. And yet, how many times do we hand our peace over to others over small matters such as being late, traffic jams, or little setbacks in our day? It is so easy to get upset and overwhelmed by the littlest things. Instead of pausing and praying and asking the Lord for his peace, we lash out in irrational anger or emotions that can destroy our peace and that of our families.

Here is one family's story of moving toward peace after enthroning the Sacred Heart in their home.

TESTIMONY FROM PEACEFUL HEARTS

After we experienced the Enthronement of the Sacred Heart, we started to notice the little things that were robbing our family of our peace. As a family, we saw that our quarrels and arguments were divisive and often only resulted from exhaustion and annoyance. Once we allowed the Sacred Heart to be the center of our home, we prioritized peaceful living. It didn't mean that our family didn't have conflict, but making sure our conflict was expressed in respectful and kind ways became a new priority. Our goal slowly became to be a household that reflected the love of Jesus.

—A Household Seeking Peace

Bringing Peace to Your Home

Our family should be our greatest gift and treasure, yet if all is not as it should be, those who should love us most can become the very people who hurt us and rob us of our security, peace, and joy. These painful experiences are all too common; more and more, children experience growing up dealing with their parents' marriage troubles and the lack of a loving, Christ-centered home. Even if we share the tenets of the faith, if the home lacks peace, we need to readjust as parents! We would not have such horrible issues in society if the fundamental cell of society, the family unit, were stronger and well insulated with Christ's peace.

Today, many homes, especially in America, are beautifully decorated, but without the peace of Christ, they can be cold and heartless. However, this is not a new phenomenon. Long before the troubles of our day, Fr. Mateo shared these concerns as his apostolic work to promote the enthronement worldwide was launched in 1907. This

Spiritual Father, full of apostolic zeal and drive, had a profound understanding that the Sacred Heart was the solution to a society growing cold and to families struggling. We are all invited to embrace the love of Christ so that we can navigate how we live our lives and learn to keep Christ at the center of our life no matter what our trials.

It is easy to believe the lies of society—that money, wealth, and power will bring happiness and peace through financial stability, influence, and success. We can be tempted to think that we would finally be at peace "if only" our jobs were more fulfilling, or we had more money or a better house. But the truth is, only Jesus can bring us peace, and we are called to share it with others in love.

Fr. Jean Croiset, St. Margaret Mary's spiritual director, wrote, "Love brings peace. The gift of self in pure love for the Sacred Heart establishes his reign of love and peace in our hearts. So closely are this love and peace connected that the enemy of peace is the very same enemy of pure love. Self-love leads to that useless reflection on self which troubles and upsets our souls. The way to peace is the exercise of pure love, a complete abandonment to God's will."[3] So with the peace of Christ, the love of Christ, and the determination to share this love with others, we can be vessels of love for all we meet in our daily interactions.

Blessed Are the Peacemakers

We must be on a mission to incorporate this profound devotion and help promote the peace of Christ to others. In the Beatitudes, we read, "Blessed are the peacemakers, / for they will be called children of God" (Mt 5:9). St. Paul wrote, "And let the peace of Christ control your hearts, the peace into which you were also called in one body. And be thankful" (Col 3:15). We are invited to be peacemakers, unifiers, and even the glue for those who are outcasts and those on the fringe of living out their faith. When we bring the peace of Christ to situations, we live out our identity as children of God, and this fundamental identity has an eternal impact.

Our personal example and outreach to others are a powerful way for us to be the hands and feet of Jesus. Fr. Francis Fernandez wrote, "We Christians have to spread the interior peace we have in our hearts, wherever we find ourselves."[4] We are invited to bring the peace of Christ to everyone we encounter with the simple gesture of a smile, a kind word, or even offering a prayer for someone suffering in pain. If we are willing to share this peace with others and be peacemakers, we are better able to be loving witnesses to what the kingdom of God looks like. If we lack inner peace and allow the pressure and anxiety of this day and age to run our lives, we miss out on being missionaries to others through sharing Christ.

Recently, I made one of my closing comments at the grocery-store checkout line: "Peace be with you." I was astounded to see the reaction. The clerk's face lit up with recognition as she responded, "And also with you." As it turns out, she was a Catholic from India who appreciated the deep and rich meaning of the words we often take for granted when we recite them in Holy Mass. Peace is the greatest gift the Lord can give us; through his heart, we can make this a defining piece of our legacy. Even those without religion or faith would agree that a more peaceful world would genuinely make a difference!

PRUDENCE: A PEACEMAKING VIRTUE THAT FLOWS FROM THE HEART OF JESUS

Prudence and prayer go hand in hand, as we are called to be people who ask the Holy Spirit to inspire us to act according to God's will in every situation. Our prudence should help us to be most effective in spreading the love of Jesus Christ and keeping the peace of Christ within our souls.

Think of your regrets at the end of the day. Often it is when you lost your cool; said something unkind; got impatient with a child; or wasted money, resources, or even time! Asking Jesus to fill you with the virtue of prudence doesn't make you a prude; it enables you to have "right judgment" in all situations. You have a clear perspective on how your actions will impact the other person versus just "lashing out."

I have written about this virtue in my book *The Friendship Project*, where I share how we are called to be "prudent" friends and how this virtue can help protect us and guide us in spiritual friendship. I have found that having Catholic friends and relationships in my life helps me grow in this virtue because we are always discerning together the best way to live out our earthly vocation.

Over the years, I have begun to see in my own life that if I act with more prudence in what I choose to share and how I share it, this will directly bring about more peace in the family. I have realized, for example, that my desire to "get everything off my chest" to my husband or children has not been bearing much peace for them. I have not always shared with kindness (an absolute necessity), having prayerfully considered the impact of my words. My laundry list of complaints can be hurtful and undermine my parenting and relationships; this lack of prudence can significantly detract from the primary goal. For example, focusing on everything wrong doesn't lead to people being "saints"; it just causes discouragement. Instead, we can focus on mentoring, parenting, or guiding others with just one primary goal and providing a load of encouragement to assist!

If we ask the Lord to make us more prudent, we will begin to see the times we might have provoked others to anger or anxiety based on our timing and wording. This virtue functions as an excellent guide, and Jesus is its source. He wants us to be wise and learn how to navigate all life situations with the Holy Spirit's help.

St. Paul counsels, "If possible, on your part, live at peace with all" (Rom 12:18). If we can master this interior disposition of Christ's peace, we will be a light shining in a dark world. It is very evident that people lack the peace of Christ by how they respond to life's circumstances. We are invited to remind ourselves and others that Jesus wants his heart to be our refuge and that we need to place our trust in him. If we can better navigate what robs us of our peace, such as being irritable from lack of sleep or too much caffeine or working too much and missing out on life balance, we can better reach this life goal recommended by St. Paul.

Prudence will help us not only fight for our inner peace but also evaluate how to live out our day-to-day life and navigate relationships. Maybe you will discover that as you grow in this powerful virtue, you will have better relationships with your family, and your children or grandchildren will start to listen to you. When others shut us out it is often because our "track record" isn't the greatest. We might have been irrational, angry, lacking good timing, or just downright dominating in conversations. When we grow in prudence, we allow the Lord to speak to our hearts and lead our discussions. A great example of this is when my great-uncle Bud mentioned that he felt like he needed to volunteer at the soup kitchen to serve the poor; he would sometimes leave upset by how the people received and reacted to the meal. Soon he realized that if he wanted to achieve any spiritual benefit, it was best for him to wash the dishes and, as a result, not analyze or judge the meal participants. He was an excellent example to me of not only knowing yourself but also being prudent in not tempting yourself to cast judgment on others.

Prudence leads to being a better listener. I recently heard an excellent talk by Msgr. John Esseff. One suggestion he made is for us to be contemplative listeners. This means don't jump to conclusions before you fully hear the other person. Instead, listen with your heart. Ask the Holy Spirit to awaken your heart so that as you listen, you are not forming your rebuttal in your head but instead allowing a dialogue to be sincere and peaceful. This type of listening requires prudence and a peaceful spirit! If we can do this, we will be able to make room for the Lord to touch our hearts and to share the love of Jesus with anyone.

Enter the School of the Sacred Heart: Be a Peacemaker

Holy scripture says, "Strive for peace with everyone, and for that holiness without which no one will see the Lord" (Heb 12:14). Who are you needing to reconcile and restore a relationship with? How can the peace of Christ and the virtue of prudence lead to personal and inherent transformation? How can this virtue help you let go of your past hurts and anger and forgive? I have seen that if we do not allow the Lord to work in our hearts, he will not be able to work in our relationships.

LET US PRAY: CONSECRATION TO THE SACRED HEART BY ST. MARGARET MARY

The prayer of the Consecration to the Sacred Heart written by St. Margaret Mary is a powerful way to connect your heart to the heart of Jesus. Just think, these are words this great saint wrote as a way to connect her heart with the heart of Jesus. When we turn to Jesus and give him the authority and power to rule in our lives, he will outdo us in kindness and protection so that we can better live out our Catholic faith. When we feel weak and weary, spiritually powerful prayers like these can ground us and help change our hearts.

> O Sacred Heart of Jesus, to Thee I consecrate and offer up my person and my life, my actions, trials, and sufferings, that my entire being may henceforth only be employed in loving, honoring, and glorifying Thee. This is my irrevocable will, to belong entirely to thee and to do all for Thy love, renouncing with my whole heart all that can displease Thee.

> I take thee, O Sacred Heart, for the sole object of my love, the protection of my life, the pledge of my salvation, the remedy of my frailty and inconstancy, the reparation for all the defects of my life,

and my secure refuge at the hour of my death.
Be Thou, O Most Merciful Heart, my justifica-
tion before God Thy Father, and screen me from
his anger which I have so justly merited. I fear all
from my own weakness and malice, but placing
my entire confidence in Thee, O Heart of Love, I
hope all from Thine infinite Goodness. Annihilate
in me all that can displease or resist Thee. Imprint
Thy pure love so deeply in my heart that I may
never forget Thee or be separated from Thee.

I beseech Thee, through Thine infinite Goodness, grant that my name be engraved upon Thy
heart, for in this I place all my happiness and all
my glory, to live and to die as one of Thy devoted
servants. Amen.[5]

REFLECTION QUESTIONS

1. How can you live out a more peaceful home life?
2. What robs you of your inner peace? Share an example
   of a time you allowed anger and frustration to rob your
   personal peace.
3. What is the connection between Christ's peace and
   being prudent?
4. How can you become a more peaceful and prudent
   person through the Sacred Heart devotion?

APPENDIX 1:
WHAT IS AN ENTHRONEMENT?

The Enthronement has been a path for many Catholic families to encounter Christ in their homes. In 1907, Fr. Mateo Crawley-Boevey had a miraculous prayer experience in the chapel of St. Margaret Mary in eastern France. He felt that the Lord was calling him to promote the Enthronement of the Sacred Heart to strengthen Catholic families and protect them from the wave of secularism and modernism. After his prayer experience, his back was healed, his health improved, and he began what would be forty years of preaching and sharing this life-changing devotion throughout the world. The Father of Enthronement, Fr. Mateo invites each Catholic to live out their faith by being transformed by the heart of Jesus.

The purpose of the enthronement is to unite your family (or "work family," "school family," or "parish family") so you can worship the Lord in one voice and build a covenant of love with the heart of Jesus. Jesus wants you to experience more love—first between him and you and next between you and others. We know that love conquers hearts, so why not begin cultivating this devotion to the heart of Jesus?

The Sacred Heart devotion takes on profound meaning when a Catholic or Catholic family engages in a spiritual process that focuses on welcoming the kingdom of

Christ through the Enthronement of the Sacred Heart of Jesus. When we read Psalm 102:13, "But you, LORD, are enthroned forever; your renown is for all generations," we see that the Lord is enthroned forever and that all generations are invited to honor and love him. Jesus will not use strength and force to change hearts; his way is kindness and love.

Jesus is our King, and he desires to be placed on the throne of our hearts. Jesus longs for us to come to invite him into our lives as King, Savior, Brother, and Friend; he wants us to welcome his kingdom into our hearts so that we can experience joy, peace, and love through building a covenant of love.

Enthronement means seating the king on his throne. Jesus is the King of all kings, and we desire to enthrone him in our hearts and homes. Jesus promised through St. Margaret Mary, "Our divine Lord assured me that He takes a singular pleasure in being honored under the figure of His Heart of flesh, the image of which He wishes to be exposed in public in order to touch the unfeeling hearts of men. He promised that He would pour out in abundance into the hearts of all those who would honor His Heart all the gifts with which it is filled, and everywhere this image is exposed and honored it would draw down all kinds of blessings."[1]

This reality can lead to not only a greater encounter with the Lord but also a deepening of faith for the entire family and those who visit the house.

For more information about enthroning the Sacred Heart in your home, visit the Sacred Heart Enthronement Network at www.welcomehisheart.com. Welcoming Jesus into your life through the Enthronement of the Sacred Heart is a way to encounter the loving heart of Jesus in your home. Exposing and honoring an image of the Sacred Heart is also a powerful way to live out the twelve promises of the Sacred Heart of Jesus (see appendix 2).

APPENDIX 2:
THE TWELVE PROMISES
OF THE
SACRED HEART OF JESUS

1. I will give them all the graces necessary in their state of life.
2. I will establish peace in their homes.
3. I will comfort them in all their afflictions.
4. I will be their secure refuge during life, and above all, in death.
5. I will bestow abundant blessings upon all their undertakings.
6. Sinners will find in My Heart the source and infinite ocean of mercy.
7. Lukewarm souls shall become fervent.
8. Fervent souls shall quickly mount to high perfection.
9. I will bless every place in which an image of My Heart is exposed and honored.
10. I will give to priests the gift of touching the most hardened hearts.
11. Those who shall promote this devotion shall have their names written in My Heart.
12. I promise you in the excessive mercy of My Heart that My all-powerful love will grant to all those who receive Holy Communion on the First Fridays in nine

consecutive months the grace of final perseverance; they shall not die in My disgrace, nor without receiving their sacraments. My divine Heart shall be their safe refuge in this last moment.

NOTES

Introduction

1. André Prévot, *Love, Peace, and Joy: Devotion to the Sacred Heart of Jecording to Saint Gertrude* (Rockford, IL: Tan Books, 1984), 2.

2. Prévot, *Love, Peace, and Joy*, 3.

1. Receive the King: Experience God's Love with Docility

1. Mateo Crawley-Boevey, *Jesus: King of Love* (Fairhaven, MA: National Enthronement Center, 1997), 132.

2. Margaret Mary Alacoque, *The Letters of St. Margaret Mary Alacoque: Apostle of the Sacred Heart*, trans. Clarence A. Herbst (Rockford, IL: Tan Books, 1997), 143.

3. Alacoque, *Letters*, 163.

4. Donald DeMarco, "The Virtue of Docility," Catholic Exchange, July 10, 2003, https://catholicexchange.com/the-virtue-of-docility/.

5. Alacoque, *Letters*, 50.

6. "Sacred Heart Prayer—Oh Most Holy Heart of Jesus," *Welcome His Heart*, February 20, 2019, https://welcomehisheart.com/o-most-holy-heart-of-jesus.

2. Welcome the Light: Overcome Shame with Faith in God's Grace

1. Alacoque, *Letters*, 146.

2. Francis Larkin, *Enthronement of the Sacred Heart* (Boston: Pauline Press, 1978), 27.

3. Larkin, *Enthronement*, 27.

4. Larkin, *Enthronement*, 33.

5. Alacoque, *Letters*, 25.

6. Peter Kreeft, "Virtues and Vices," in *How Catholics Live*, part 3, section 4, Catholic Christianity series, ed. John A. Farren (New Haven, CT: Knights of Columbus Supreme Council, 2001), 10.

7. Bernardine of Siena (d. 1444), from a Good Friday Sermon, quoted in Larkin, *Enthronement*, 538.

3. Make Yours a House of Prayer: Build Fortitude with Jesus

1. Alacoque, *Letters*, 164.

2. Larkin, *Enthronement*, 28.

3. Larkin, *Enthronement,* 31.

4. Larkin, *Enthronement*, 33.

5. Carol Kennedy and Dominic Rasmussen, *Remain in Me, Faith Formation Curriculum* (Ann Arbor, MI: Spiritus Sanctus Publications, 2001), 120.

6. "Fortitude," Catholic News Agency, accessed July 13, 2022, https://www.catholicnewsagency.com/resource/55557/fortitude.

7. Anne Costa, *Healing Promises: The Essential Guide to the Sacred Heart* (Cincinnati, OH: Franciscan Media, 2017), 185.

4. Establish Christ as Your Center: Find Spiritual Stability through Hope

1. Alacoque, *Letters*, 140.

2. Josemaría Escrivá, *Furrow* (New York: Scepter, 1987), chap. 27, "Peace," no. 864. Available at https://www.escrivaworks.org/book/furrow-point-864.htm.

3. Francis Fernandez, *In Conversation with God* (Princeton, NJ: Scepter, 1997), 3:519.

4. Larkin, *Enthronement*, 542.

5. Cultivate Compassion: Awaken Charity in Your Heart

1. Alacoque, *Letters*, 129.

2. Margaret Mary Alacoque, *Thoughts and Sayings of St. Margaret Mary for Every Day of the Year*, trans. Sisters of the Visitation (Rockford, IL: Tan Books, 1986), 87.

3. Mateo Crawley-Boevey, *20 Holy Hours* (Fairhaven, MA: National Enthronement Center, 2013), 90.

4. Alacoque, *Letters*, 164.

5. Alacoque, *Letters*, 7.

6. Alacoque, *Letters*, 94.

7. Larkin, *Enthronement*, 540.

6. Let Go of Control: Grow in Meekness and Humility

1. Alacoque, *Thoughts and Sayings*, 89.

2. Margaret Mary Alacoque, *The Autobiography of Saint Margaret Mary* (Rockford, IL: Tan Books, 1986), 123.

3. St. John Paul II, Apostolic Letter *Novo millenio ineunte* (January 6, 2001), 32.

4. Josemaría Escrivá, *Friends of God: Homilies by Josemaría Escrivá* (New Delhi: Scepter India, 1997), no. 242.

5. Alacoque, *Letters*, xx.

6. Margaret Mary Alacoque, "A Prayer in Resignation to Suffering," Catholic Doors, accessed February 13, 2023, https://www.catholicdoors.com/prayers/english2/p01018.htm.

7. Put Jesus in Your Relationships: The Gift of Forgiveness

1. Alacoque, *Thoughts and Sayings*, 64.

2. Alacoque, *Letters*, 164.

3. Alacoque, *Thoughts and Sayings*, 47.

4. Crawley-Boevey, *Jesus: King of Love*, 77.

5. John Chrysostom, *The Homilies of S. John Chrysostom, Archbishop of Constantinople, on the Gospel of St. Matthew,* trans. George Prevost (London: Walter Smith, 1885), 300.

6. "Prayers to the Sacred Heart," Franciscan Media, accessed July 22, 2022, https://www.franciscanmedia.org/franciscan-spirit-blog/prayers-to-the-sacred-heart.

8. Break Attachments and Addictions: The Power of Temperance and Self-Control

1. Jean Croiset, *The Devotion to the Sacred Heart of Jesus: How to Practice the Sacred Heart Devotion,* trans. Patrick O'Connell (Rockford, IL: Tan Books, 1988), 80.

2. Editor's note: Spiritual direction, Confession, and counseling can all be useful in helping a person "detach" from unhealthy habits. However, those who struggle with substance abuse and other serious addictions should consult with a medical doctor to decide the best course of treatment.

3. Alacoque, *Thoughts and Sayings*, 95.

4. Mary C. Darrah, *Sister Ignatia: Angel of Alcoholics Anonymous* (Center City, MN: Hazelden Pittman Archives Press, 2001), 105.

5. Darrah, *Sister Ignatia*, 106.

6. Croiset, *Devotion to the Sacred Heart*, 243.

7. Alacoque, *Thoughts and Sayings*, 86.

8. Crawley-Boevey, *Jesus: King of Love*, 93.

9. "A Prayer for Daily Neglects: Offering the Sacred Heart of Jesus," Our Catholic Prayers, accessed January 11, 2023, www.ourcatholicprayers.com/prayer-for-daily-neglects.html.

9. Expand the Kingdom: Practice Joy and Gratitude

1. Alacoque, *Thoughts and Sayings*, 87.

2. Alacoque, *Letters*, 164.

3. Crawley-Boevey, *Jesus: King of Love*, 93.

4. Alacoque, *Thoughts and Sayings*, 49.

5. Alacoque, *Thoughts and Sayings*, 49.

6. Alacoque, *Letters*, 101.

7. Crawley-Boevey, *20 Holy Hours*, 92.

8. Fernandez, *In Conversation with God*, 2:442.

9. Alacoque, *Letters*, 101.

10. Alacoque, *Thoughts and Sayings*, 49.

11. Msgr. John Esseff, personal interview by Emily Jaminet, August 2022.

12. Larkin, *Enthronement*, 535, quoting from *The Raccolta*, no. 260.

10. Live in the Kingdom of Peace: Let Prudence Guide You

1. Alacoque, *Thoughts and Sayings*, 34.

2. Alacoque, *Letters*, 39.

3. Croiset, *Devotion to the Sacred Heart*, xv.

4. Fernandez, *In Conversation with God*, 1:20.

5. Margaret Mary Alacoque, "Consecration to the Sacred Heart," *The Catholic Crusade*, accessed July 26, 2022, https://www.thecatholiccrusade.com/consecration-to-the-sacred-heart-by-saint-margaret-mary-alacoque.html.

Appendix 1

1. Larkin, *Enthronement*, 78.

Emily Jaminet is the executive director of the Sacred Heart Enthronement Network. She is the author of the award-winning book *Secrets of the Sacred Heart* and the coauthor of *Divine Mercy for Moms*, *The Friendship Project*, *Pray Fully*, and *Our Friend Faustina*.

Jaminet earned a bachelor's degree in mental health and human services from Franciscan University of Steubenville in 1998. She is the cohost of *Inspired by Faith* on St. Gabriel Radio and the host of the *Emily Jaminet Podcast*. She has spoken to a number of parish and diocesan women's groups and conferences, serves on the leadership team of the Columbus Catholic Women's Conference, and consults with the Catholic Men's Ministry. She is the director of adult faith formation and coordinates RCIA for her parish.

Jaminet has appeared on EWTN's *Women of Grace*, *Bookmark*, and *At Home with Jim and Joy*. She is a monthly contributor on Spirit Catholic Radio, Relevant Radio, and Diocesan. com. She also writes for CatholicMom.com.

Jaminet received the Bishop John King Mussio Award from Franciscan University. She and her husband, John, have seven children and live in Columbus, Ohio.

www.emilyjaminet.com
welcomehisheart.com
inspirethefaith.com
Facebook: Emily Jaminet - A Mother's Moment
Instagram: @_EmilyJaminet

ALSO BY
EMILY JAMINET

Secrets of the Sacred Heart
Twelve Ways to Claim Jesus' Promises in Your Life
Emily Jaminet takes up each of the twelve promises Christ
made to St. Margaret Mary Alacoque, puts a fresh, new spin
on the classic Catholic devotion, and invites you and your family
to experience the profound spiritual benefits you will receive when
you keep the Sacred Heart of Jesus at the center of your home.

Divine Mercy for Moms
Sharing the Lessons of St. Faustina
In *Divine Mercy for Moms*, Michele Faehnle and Emily Jaminet break
open the history, practices, and prayers associated with the devotion,
guiding busy moms to receive God's message of Divine Mercy
and pass it on to others through their words, deeds, and prayers.

The Friendship Project
The Catholic Woman's Guide to Making
and Keeping Fabulous, Faith-Filled Friends
Drawing on the cardinal and theological virtues, stories of the saints,
and anecdotes from their own friendships, Michele Faehnle
and Emily Jaminet provide a practical primer for any Catholic woman
seeking ways to deepen old friendships and develop new ones of virtue.

Pray Fully
Simple Steps for Becoming a Woman of Prayer
In *Pray Fully*, Michele Faehnle and Emily Jaminet share the rewards
and frustrations of their own prayer journeys to create
a practical guide that combines testimonies, tips, and journaling
space to help you spend quality time with God.